ROMANCE OF THE
GOLCONDA DIAMONDS

Diamonds

Omar Khalidi

Mapin Publishing Pvt. Ltd.

First published in
the United States of America in 1999
by
Grantha Corporation
80 Cliffedgeway, Middletown,
NJ 07701

in association with
Mapin Publishing Pvt. Ltd.
Chidambaram, Ahmedabad 380013
India

Distributed in North America by
Antique Collectors' Club
Market Street, Industrial Park
Wappingers' Falls, NY 12590
Tel: 800-252-5321 Fax: 914-297-0068
Web-site: www.antiquecc.com

Distributed in the United Kingdom &
Europe by
Antique Collectors' Club
5 Church Street, Woodbridge
Suffolk IP12 1DS
Tel: 1394-385-501 Fax: 1394-384-434
Email: accvs@aol.com

Text and photographs
© Omar Khalidi
except when noted otherwise

ISBN: 1-890206-10-5
ISBN: 81-85822-57-3
LC: 98-87558

Edited by: Mallika Sarabhai
Designed by: Amit Kharsani /
Mapin Design Studio
Colour separations by & printed at
Ajanta Offset, New Delhi

Frontispiece
Ahmedabad diamond
© Christies's Images New York

ACKNOWLEDGEMENTS

During the four years spent in the research and writing of this book, I have received encouragement and practical help from a number of people. Foremost, my wife Nigar Sultana, who relieved me of all family responsibilities in order for me to concentrate on the book. Her share in the successful completion of this project is far more than she realises. Murtaza and Habiba Baig treated me with warm hospitality in London during the research. I have benefited from the informed comments and suggestions of Shahzadah Mufakhkham Jah, Lord Ian Balfour and Susan Stronge, the leading authority on the Mogul jewellery at the Victoria & Albert Museum. For geological information, I am indebted to Dr. M. Nasib.

Quraishi and Krishna Brahmam, both of the National Geophysical Research Institute in Hyderabad. A number of institutions provided images, including *Siyasat* newspaper in Hyderabad; Los Angeles County Museum of Natural History; Aramco Services Co., Houston, Texas; National Jewellery Museum, Tehran; Royal Ontario Museum, Toronto; Biblioth,que Nationale and Louvre Museum, Paris; Christie's Images and Sotheby's, New York, and Dar al-Athar al-Islamiyya, Kuwait. Among the jewellery companies, De Beers, Henell of Bond Street, and Graff Diamonds Ltd, all located in London supplied a number of illustrations. Other individuals who helped me in various ways are Muhammad Nizam.

Mohiuddin (Hyderabad); Dr. Abusalman Shahjahanpuri (Karachi); Zuabir Nurulhaq (Houston); Shahid Malik Khan, (Toronto); Ambassador Iradj Amini of Iran and Aminah T. Muhammad (Paris). The publisher and the staff at Mapin were most cooperative with me. To all of them, my deep felt *shukriya* !

Hyderabad, Deccan
June 17, 1997

Contents

Prologue

المـاس ولعل وسنگِ یشَب، نقرۂ و طِلا   نیلم، عقیق، سَنگِ سیه اور کوئیلا
پکھراج، سنگِ مرمر و یاقوتِ باصفا   بلّور، هَس، حدید، نمک، جست، سنکھیا
کانیں ہیں ان کی ارضِ دکن میں دبی ہوئی
یہ دولتیں ہیں پاؤں کے نیچے گڑی ہوئی

Diamond, ruby, jasper, silver and gold
Sapphires, agates, blackstone, and coal
Topaz, marble, and the beautiful hyacinth
Glass, jade, iron, salt, zinc, and arsenic
Mines of such elements lie buried in the land of the Deccan
Wealth of great proportions lies underneath our feet.

Thus writes an anonymous Urdu poet about the mineral wealth of the Deccan in which Golconda is located.

During my first visit to England in the summer of 1979, I had the pleasure of seeing the Koh-i-Noor diamond in the Tower of London. After paying sixty pence and waiting almost half-an-hour, I descended into the New Jewel House beneath Wakefield Tower. The security was awesome: two-way mirrors, complex electronic surveillance equipment, a two-feet-thick Chubb vault door and handsomely dressed guards in long flared coats and black top hats everywhere. There, like a tamed giant, the Koh-i-Noor rested in its velvet-lined case, boxed in bulletproof glass, locked in by careful hands, guarded by hired trustees, its beauty exposed to any passing tourist.

Standing there, looking into it, I found myself in both triumph and frustration. My heart pounded exultantly: "Here it is: the Mountain of Light." I was overcome by its sheer brilliance and beauty. Soon, however, the feeling of triumph gave way to frustration. "Why am I seeing the great diamond of the Deccan in London, and why not in either the Salar Jang Museum or the State Museum in Hyderabad?"

I was overwhelmed by the same feeling as I saw one by one the famous Deccani diamonds in the great museums in Paris, Moscow, Washington, DC and Tehran. What happened to the famous diamonds and the diamond mines of Golconda so celebrated in romance and legend? Why are the Koh-i-Noor and other fabulous diamonds no longer in the Deccan where they were found in the first place? Why do most of the known Deccani diamonds have European and not Persian or Telugu names? Who spirited away these gems of my country's natural heritage to the European and American capital cities? Why is the Hope diamond in the Smithsonian Institution in Washington D.C.; the Regent diamond in the Louvre Museum in Paris; the Orloff and the Shah in the State Armoury Museum at a Kremlin in Moscow; the Darya-i Noor in the Central Bank of Iran in Tehran, and the Jacob diamond in the Reserve Bank of India in New Delhi? What happened to the incredible wealth of the Nizam of Hyderabad, his wagon-loads of gold and silver? My fascination with the famed Golconda diamonds and the famous wealth of the Nizam led to rigorous research using Qutb Shahi and Asaf Jahi state papers in Persian and Urdu, contemporary histories, European travellers' accounts, modern academic works, and visits to the sites of the long-defunct mines. This book is the culmination of this fascinating and often disheartening search.

Romance of the Diamonds

The story of the diamond begins in a remote era of the world's history, lost in the mists of time. For untold ages the diamond lay hidden and unseen within the earth, until Homo Sapiens at last recognised it as the most precious of all nature's creations and began to use it for his own delight and benefit. For over 3000 years the small pieces of rock called diamonds have excited the wonder, interest, and envy of humanity, from the richest to the most destitute. They have aroused interest in the historian and the folklorist, the industrialist and the businessman, the scientist and the technologist, the speculator and the investor, the craftsperson and the artist. Many diamonds are linked to strange histories —often stranger than fiction. For several centuries diamonds have appeared in royal treasuries, temples, and in the minds of the commoners. Men and women have killed for them. Countries have flourished and regimes have fallen because of them. Diamonds have always been far more than jewels: they are fragments of history twinkling on the skin. Probably no one will ever know exactly when or where the first diamonds were discovered. But one thing we know is that from ancient times until the 18th century, India, and especially the Deccan, was the world's sole supplier of this most coveted of all stones.

Diamonds in Legend, Romance, and Ancient Literature

The ancient Sanskrit treatise by Kautilya called the *Artha Shastra* or "The Science of Profit" is a basic text providing invaluable details of the economic, political and legal system of India in the fourth century B.C. Kautilya was a minister of Emperor Chandragupta Maurya and had helped him to the throne of Magadha in what is now the north Indian state of Bihar. In the chapter on "The Examination of Precious Articles to Be Received in the Treasury," Kautilya describes the sources of diamonds ("in mines and streams"); the most valuable diamonds ("those that are big, crystalline and brilliant"); diamonds considered the least valuable ("those that are devoid of angles and are uneven," i.e. diamond splinters); and the various colours of diamonds ("like cat's eye or the urine or bile of a cow"). Also described are the octahedral shape of diamond crystals. The treatise also suggests a strict control over trade in gems!

Another classical Sanskrit work, written by Buddhabhatta called the *Ratnapariksha*, Appreciation of Gems, is a compilation of Indian traditions about precious stones, their varieties, qualities, and sources, apparently written as a technical manual before the sixth century A.D. The compendium expressly states that the best form in which to have a diamond is as a perfect natural octahedral crystal and not as a cut stone, with the clear implication that cutting was already a well-known practice. Yet another text, the *Brihatsamhita* of Varahamihira dating from about the same time, offers similar insights.

In the history of India, the campaign of Alexander the Great is the earliest event that can be dated with certainty. In 327 B.C. Alexander set out from Bactria and Sogdiana with 100,000 men. He followed the valley of Kabul and in the spring of the following year reached the banks of the Indus, the border of the country of five rivers. The campaign, though short, exhausted the army, and the Greek invader was forced to withdraw to Persepolis. In the wake of his Indian invasion, Alexander left behind an interesting legend.

This is the story of how Alexander the Great ventured into a diamond pit, a tale told by a man who claimed to be Aristotle's nephew and a companion of Alexander on his campaign through India. Reportedly, the diamond pit was guarded by snakes and the snakes had a gaze of such fatal power that when they looked upon a man he died. This did not deter Alexander for long. He outwitted the snakes with mirrors held in front of his men like so many shields. When the snakes gazed into the mirrors their fatal gaze was turned upon themselves and they died. Now Alexander himself peered into the pit and, seeing the diamonds there, ordered his men to throw down the carcasses of freshly slain sheep. The diamonds adhered to the fat of the flesh and the flesh lured vultures. Soon the sky was filled with the great birds who, swooping down, seized the diamond-studded flesh and soared skyward. Beneath them Alexander's men ran, picking up the diamonds that fell and following the vultures to their mountain roosts to garner the rest.

A remarkably similar story is told in the Islamic tradition. In the Second Voyage, Sindbad the Sailor recalls his descent into the Valley of Diamonds after being cast by the giant bird Roc into an inaccessible valley that is lined with diamonds but also inhabited by snakes. The scene has been copied by film-makers from Cecil B. de Mille to Steven Spielberg:
"The soil was of diamonds but swarmed with mighty snakes from which I sought refuge in a cave. Within was another serpent, brooding her eggs. I passed the night with her, in great fear. Staggering in the morning with hunger, terror, and fatigue, I ventured forth, and a big piece of meat dropped before me. Now, I had heard that diamond merchants cast freshly flayed sheep into the valley of diamonds, the meat being sticky, jewels cling to it; then vultures and eagles swoop and carry the meat to the mountain tops,

"This is the valley of diamonds," says the Ottoman-Turkish miniature in manuscript dated 1582. It is guarded by serpents with a lethal gaze. Overhead, birds of prey carry lumps of meat to which diamonds adhere. © Bibliotheque Nationale

where the merchants scare them away and collect the jewels.

"Therefore I quickly filled my clothes with diamonds, tied to meat across my chest, and lay on my back. An eagle lifted me to the mountains, where a man, shouting, drove him off; but the man was himself startled when he beheld me there. I gave him some of the diamonds and told my tale." Several centuries after the Arabian Nights were composed, Venetian traveller Marco Polo, the first cultured European to journey across Asia in the late thirteenth century, wrote a detailed account of his adventures. In his *Book of Marvels*, he repeated the Sindbad legend about the diamonds.

H. Rider Haggard imitated the scene in King Solomon's Mines, and so did John Buchan, author of *The 39 Steps*. Both authors were veterans of the diamond fields. "The whole of my stones I sold to De Beers," says the adventurous hero of Prester John, "for if I had placed them on the open market I should have upset the delicate equipoise of diamond values. When I came finally to cast up my accounts, I found that I had secured a fortune of a trifle over a quarter of a million pounds. The wealth did not dazzle so much as it solemnized me. I had no impulse to spend any part of it in a riot of folly... It had been bought with men's blood..." A 1921 American movie The Hope Diamond Mystery, directed by Paton Stuart, follows the story of the Hope diamond, beginning in the 16th century, and shows the tragedies it brings to those who are involved with it until it is returned to its rightful place in the breast of a Hindu idol representing the god of love.

Similarly, in *The Moonstone*, England's first detective story, Wilkie Collins speaks of an enormous yellow diamond, plucked from the forehead of a Hindu deity and possessed by a series of unfortunate owners from India to Britain and back again. "This jewel that you could hold between your finger and thumb seemed as unfathomable as the heavens themselves. We set it in the sun, and then shut the light out of the room, and it shone awfully out of the depths of its own brightness.... No wonder Miss Rachel was fascinated; no wonder her cousins screamed... The only one of us who kept his senses was Mr. Godfrey. He put an arm around each of his sisters' waists, and, looking compassionately backwards and forwards between the diamond and me, said, "Carbon, Betteridge! mere carbon, my good friends after all." Mere carbon; mere fiction. The truth about diamonds—particularly those found in the Golconda mines— is, as we shall see, much more exotic.

Sinbad carried off by the roc. Illustration by H. J. Ford, 19th century.
Source: *Arabian Nights Entertainment,* edited by Andrew Lang, (London: Longmans, 1898)

Top left
Sinbad in the valley of serpents. Illustration by H. J. Ford, 19th century.
Source: Unknown

The Nature of Diamonds

Physical Properties

A diamond is the hardest naturally-occurring substance and also one of the most valuable. It is the only gemstone composed of a single element. Because of its hardness, the diamond is the most lasting of all gemstones. Diamonds are crystals made up entirely of carbon. Some diamond crystals have six faces, but most form octahedrons, with eight faces. Other crystal shapes also occur, some of which are very complex. Natural diamonds probably form in the earth's upper mantle—the zone beneath the crust—where high temperature and pressure cause the diamonds to crystallise. The diamonds are later brought to the earth's surface by volcanic activity. A diamond will not dissolve in acid, but it can be destroyed when it is subjected to intense heat. If a diamond is heated in the presence of oxygen it will burn and form carbon-dioxide. If it is heated without oxygen, a diamond will turn to graphite, a form of carbon so soft that it is used as a lubricant.

Size and Colour

The size of a diamond is determined by its weight in carats. One carat equals 200 milligrams. In Golconda, the diamonds were measured in *manjali*, a Telugu word Europeanised as mangellin. *Manjali* is a seed weighing about four grains and, like *ratti*, used as a weight unit for gemstones. One *manjali* equals 1 1/3 carat, and a *ratti* equals 1 1/8 carat. Diamonds vary from colourless to black and they may be transparent, translucent or opaque. Most diamonds used as gems are transparent and colourless or nearly so. Colourless or pale blue stones are most valued but these are rare, most gem diamonds are tinged with yellow. A 'fancy' diamond has a distinct body colour. Red, blue, and green are rarest; orange, violet, yellow, and yellowish-green more common. According to Benjamin Zuker, a noted gem merchant and scholar "Judging a diamond's colour is an art for the connoisseur that takes many years of experience to perfect. Even then, the Gem Institute of America has found it best to have two or three opinions before a certificate is issued. A D-colour diamond is like a piece of ice in a glass of water sitting on a gem dealer's table in Bombay on a bright, sunny day. It has a transparency and whiteness that is incredibly pure, and is so rare that no more than one in a thousand diamonds would possess that quality. White as that is, however, the old Golconda stones were by comparison 'whiter than white.' Place a Golconda diamond from an old piece of jewellery alongside a modern, recently cut D-colour diamond, and the purity of the Golconda stone will become evident."

Cutting, Faceting, and Polishing

Diamonds have great power to reflect light, blend rays of light and break light up into the colours of the rainbow, but to produce the greatest possible brilliance in a diamond, many little facets or sides must be cut and polished on it. Each tiny facet must be exactly the right size and shape and must be placed at exactly the right angle in relation to other facets.

It is only when a rough diamond is faceted that its brilliance and beauty are revealed to the eye. A diamond must be used to cut another diamond, hence the expression "diamond cut diamond!" However, a diamond can be cleanly broken with a sharp accurate blow because of its cleavage. Cleavage is a property some minerals have of splitting in certain directions and producing flat, even surfaces.

During the 1400s, diamond cutters learned how to shape and polish a stone by using an iron wheel coated with diamond dust. As people learned more about diamonds, they discovered the shapes that gave the greatest brilliance. The style of cut often seen today is the round shape with 58 facets, which is called the brilliant. This style of cutting was begun in the 1600s. Diamond saws cut diamond crystals with great accuracy, and so help prevent waste. Cutting and polishing a rough diamond is a slow and costly process. It must be done by highly trained workers who take many years to learn their trade. Indian cuts of diamond are totally different from Western ones.

Where Diamonds are Found

The first diamonds were found thousands of years ago in the sand gravel deposits of stream beds. Diamonds found in such deposits are called alluvial diamonds. Until the 18th century India in general, and the Deccan in particular, was the most important source of diamonds. In 1725 the Minas Gerais (General Mines) of Brazil were discovered and exploited by the Portuguese, taking the lead in world production from ca. 1740 until the discovery of the South African mines in the 19th century. The discovery of the first diamond on the banks of the Orange River in 1867 led to the Kimberley diamond rush and the supremacy of South Africa in the diamond trade. Under the impetus of Cecil Rhodes, production was

India (pre-1947) Diamond Locations. Map by Anne Gibson, Cartography Lab, Clark University, Worcester, Mass; 1998, based on a GSI map by W. King & R. B. Foote, Calcutta, 1881

centralised in the De Beers company founded in 1880. At the end of the 19th century, the Diamond Syndicate was formed with the object of controlling the supply of the diamonds to the market and stabilizing the relations between supply and demand. Further centralisation was achieved with the formation of the Diamond Producers' Association in 1933 and the Diamond Trading Company in 1934, by which virtually worldwide control of the diamond industry was secured. De Beers coined the motto "Diamonds are Forever" to sell the precious stone that it has controlled worldwide for a century and more. The slogan could well apply to the South African-based mining company itself. Its multi-million dollar advertising campaign polishes the myth that diamonds should not be resold but held onto forever. For instance, new markets have been created in the Far East where De Beers single-handedly changed courtship rituals by introducing the European tradition of engagement diamonds. Today Africa, Australia, and Russia in all produce about 97 percent of the world output of diamonds. In comparison, India is an insignificant source of diamonds today. However, our concern is with the historic diamond mines located in the Deccan, to which we now turn.

Golconda Diamond Mines in the Krishna and Godavari districts of Andhra Pradesh. Map by W. T. Blandford, W. King, & R. B. Foote, GSI, Calcutta, 1881

Right
Karnul Diamond Mines. Map by W. King and R. B. Foote, GSI, Calcutta, 1881

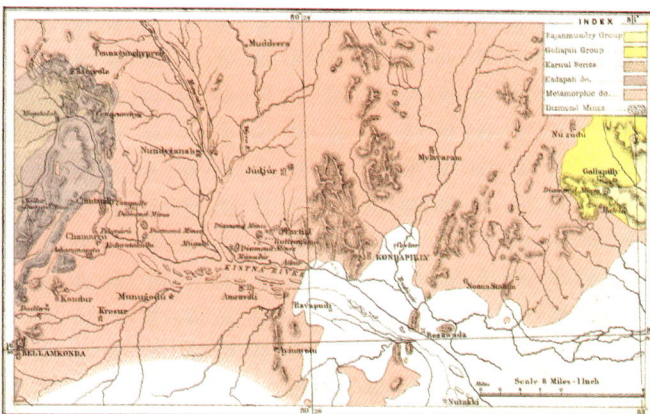

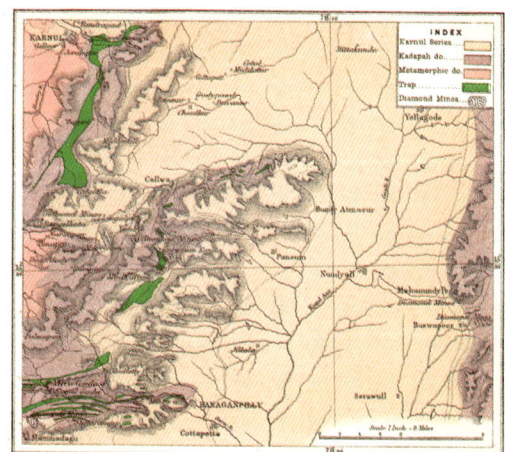

Golconda:
The Legend and the History

Golconda! What a name to conjure up in the world of diamonds. The very word is associated with fabulous wealth, bejewelled princes and horses, turbaned traders and covered oriental bazaars, tales of romance and chivalry, of Qutb Shahi and Mogul harems guarded by sword- wielding Abyssinian eunuchs, and soldiers mounted on fine Arabian steeds. In short, the ambiance in the Qutb Shahi fort of Golconda was the closest an Indian could experience of the distant yet familiar scenes of the *Alf Layla wa layla*, the Thousand and One Arabian Nights.

Golconda has been celebrated in both fiction and fact as a virtual El Dorado. Several towns in the Western world are named after its fabulous wealth. Thus, in the United States, there is Golconda, Illinois, in the Midwest, and Golconda, Colorado and Nevada in the West. The founders of the American towns hoped that great riches would flow from the mineral wealth of these areas. Unfortunately the optimism of the founders did not result in real wealth coming to their towns though they are located in romantic settings in the same manner as the original Golconda. In Tasmania, a province of Australia, there is yet another Golconda, a legacy of the miners' hope of finding diamonds down under! Across continents in distant Stockholm, the leading Swedish musician Franz Berwald (1796-1868) composed his major opera called Queen of Golconda in the mid-19th century. In the Minas Gerais group of diamond mines in Brazil, there is a Golconda mine as well as one named Coromandel after the coastal region of the Golconda kingdom. The Indian names were given

Golconda Mine, Minas Gerais, Brazil. Photograph by A.R. Kampf, Los Angeles County Museum of Natural History, 1987

Below left
Golconda towns in the United States

Below centre
Golconda, Tasmania, Australia

Below right
Golconda and Coromandel Diamond Mines, Minas Gerais, Brazil

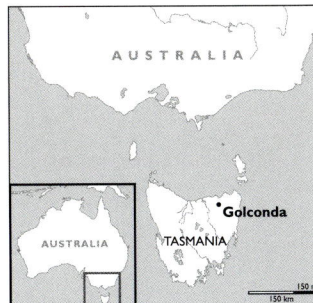

All three Maps by Anne Gibson, Cartography Lab, Clark University, Worcester, Mass; 1998

by the Portuguese familiar with the jewel trade via Goa, their outpost on the western coast. A large number of novels, plays, musical scores, and the like are named Golconda. Several films are based on stories of famous diamonds of Golconda such as the Hope Diamond and the Idol's Eye. A keyword search on WorldCat, an electronic database of books reveals an astonishing 200-plus titles available in libraries worldwide in the Autumn of 1997. The titles included sober business histories such as Black Golconda: the Romance of Petroleum and Once in Golconda, in addition to the numerous fictional and poetical works in a number of foreign languages. Indeed, it seems that books in European languages far outnumber the titles in Urdu and Telugu, the main languages of the Golconda region.

Where exactly is Golconda located and what is its history? Golconda is the name of a huge mud fort dating back to the times of the ancient rajas of Warangal. In the fourteenth century it became part of the Deccan province of the Delhi sultans. Later it came under the control of the Bahmani empire in 1495, and upon its dissolution, achieved fame and prominence as the seat of the Qutb Shahi sultans, also called the Golconda kings. The Moguls conquered it in 1687 and later it came under the control of the Nizams of Hyderabad, who in turn were removed by the New Delhi government in September 1948.

The fort and the Qutb Shahi tomb complex associated with it are located 7 miles west of the historic city of Hyderabad, Deccan. The fort, now in ruins due to the destructive siege of 1687, is under the administrative charge of the Archaeological Survey of India.

Golconda: A Brief History

Muhammad Quli-Qutb Shah. Deccani miniature. *Indian Painting 1525-1825,* catalogued by Terence McInerney. London: David Carritt, n.d.

In the chequered history of India, while Delhi has been the symbol of power, it was always the Deccan (or the South) which was the glittering prize. The Deccan, rich in tresures, was the attraction for all the early invaders from the north and the north-west. To it first came the nine unholy Nandas, who were ancient Aryan rulers. Then came the Maurya

Left
Ibrahim Adil Shah I of Bijapur, Deccani Painting, Bijapur school, © 1590-95. Paint & gold on paper. Collection: Maharaja of Bikaner

Below
Golconda Fort, view of Bala Hissaar. Collection: Aramco, Houston, Texas

conqueror Bindusara, who had a passion for fruit and learning and who wrote to Antiochus I, the Greek ruler of the Kabul Valley, to send him a parcel of figs and a savant! Next came Ashoka, perhaps the most civilised and the greatest of the conquerors, whose famous column with the lions of Sarnath carved on it was adopted centuries later by India's national leaders as the emblem of free India. Ashoka taught India its first lesson in non-violence. On fifty-six specified days in the year killing under any pretext was categorically forbidden. Breach of this order, even to the extent of preparing a chicken broth, made the offender liable to capital punishment.

So they came to the Deccan one by one; first the Nandas, then the Mauryas, then centuries of confusion. Next came the Muslim sultans. Of these it was Alauddin, the second of the Khiljis, who first cast an acquisitive eye at the Deccan. From his first raid he brought back bags of pearls, precious stones, hundreds of elephants, thousands of horses and a Dravidian mistress, as part of his booty. He then elevated his trusted slave Malik Kafur to the rank of general and sent him on three expeditions to the Deccan. These expeditions were not strictly military. At the top of the Order of Battle which he received from his sultan, Malik Kafur found the directive, 'Find my mistress's daughter.'

The girl was found. She was wandering like an existentialist amidst the exotic carvings of the Ellora caves when the soldiers of Malik Kafur picked her up. Quickly she was dispatched to the sultan while Malik Kafur stayed behind to pick up his haul of booty, which included 2,750 pounds of gold, chests of jewels, over 300 elephants, 20,000 horses and a camel. History records that the defeated Warangal raja, Ballala III, was stripped of everything except his sacred thread.

Time washed the Khiljis out of the pages of Indian history and a new Muslim family, the Tughluqs, held sway over the capital. Muhammad bin Tughluq, the second of the dynasty, was so fascinated by the Deccan that he shifted his capital from Delhi to Devagiri, renaming it Daulatabad, or

Left
Golconda Fort, view of Bala Hissar. Photography by Aramco, Houston, Texas, n.d.

Right
Golconda Fort. Photograph by Omar Khalidi, 1996

the city of the realm, a distance of some six hundred miles. After a few years, the eccentric king moved back to imperial Delhi.

In 1347, Hasan, a dissatisfied noble of the Tughluqs, proclaimed independence of the Deccan from the Delhi sultan and founded the Bahmani Empire. The Bahmani Empire was a contemporary of the kingdom of Vijayanagara, in the southeast Deccan. The Bahmanis ruled a vast territory divided into five provinces. It was a rich and resourceful kingdom, where artists and architects, poets and scholars, military experts, and talents of all kinds were patronised from within the realm to the farthest corners of the Islamic world. Thus, architects from Central Asia and Iran built the splendid *madrasa* of Mahmud Gawan at Bidar, and poets of Hafiz Shirazi's stature accepted invitations to the royal court. In the early sixteenth century, (AD 1518) the Bahmani Empire split into five sultanates, two of which, the Adil Shahi kingdom of Bijapur in the southwest and the Qutb Shahi kingdom of Golconda in the southeast achieved worldwide fame as centres of enormous wealth, lavish patronage of Islamic learning, where arts of various kinds flourished. The two kingdoms lasted until their absorption into the Mogul Empire toward the close of the seventeenth century.

The Qutb Shahi kingdom of Golconda was spread over what is today the state of Andhra Pradesh. It was in Golconda that most of the famous diamond mines were located, though some were found in the Bijapur kingdom whose territories now form part of Karnataka. The appellation "Golconda Diamond Mines" led some to think that the mines may have been located within or around the fort of Golconda. But actually the mines that produced the famous diamonds were located in the territories of the Kingdom of Golconda and not in the fort. As the fort contained the royal palace, the treasury and the mansions of the nobility, a bazaar called Caravan-i sahu sprang up in the vicinity of the fort where the diamonds were traded. A balance to weigh diamonds, on display at the museum within the Golconda, testifies to this.

The Diamond Mines of Golconda

The fame of Golconda was not without foundation and reports began to circulate from the time of the Venetian traveller Marco Polo (1254-1324) about the existence of the mines. He visited the kingdom of Warangal around 1292, ruled at the time by Queen Rudrama Devi. According to Marco Polo, "there are certain lofty mountains in those parts; and when the winter rains fall, which are very heavy, the waters come roaring down the mountains in great torrents. When the rains are over and the waters from the mountains have ceased to flow, they search the beds of the torrents and find plenty of diamonds. In summer also there are plenty to be found in the mountains, but the heat of the sun is so great that it is scarcely possible to go thither, nor is there a drop of water to be found." Marco Polo then goes on to relate the well-known story of another way in which these diamonds were obtained, by throwing pieces of meat into deep valleys, from which they were again brought up to the mountain tops with diamonds adhering to them, by large eagles. "No country but this," he says, produces diamonds. Those which are brought to our part of the world are only the refuse, as it were, of the finer and larger stones. For the flower of the diamonds and other large gems, as well as the largest pearls, are all carried to the Great Khan and other kings and princes of those regions. In truth they possess all the treasures of the world." The Venetian traveller's remarks were confirmed by his fellow countryman, Niccolo de Conti, who travelled to the East in the fifteenth century. Describing the process of diamond mining, he relates how in hill districts infested by snakes, diamonds were found. "At certain periods of the year men bring oxen and drive them to the top of the hill, and having cut them up in pieces, cast the warm and bleeding fragments upon the summit of the other mountain. The diamonds stick to these fragments. Then come the vultures and eagles which seizing the meat for their food, fly away with it to places where they may be safe from serpents. To these places afterwards come men and collect the diamonds."

Less colourful stories came from more sober accounts. According to Rafiuddin Ibrahim Shirazi, a Persian historian of the Adil Shahis, diamonds were mined in the Bijapur kingdom and many "brought bad luck", particularly those coming from the treasure of the Vijayanagara rajas. The Russian traveller Afanasii Nikitin, who lived in the Deccan between ca. 1466-72, reported diamond mining in rocky mountains near Raichur where the diamonds are sold for " 2000 gold pounds a cubit if new or at 10, 000 if old!" Two Portuguese colonial officials around 1521 wrote about Vijayanagara, whose territories later became part of the Bijapur and Golconda sultanates. According to Fernao Nunes and Domingos Paes, "diamond mines… were farmed out on condition that all stones above twenty mangellins were sent to the raja for his personal use". An important and revealing remark is made by Nunes when he refers to one of the chief officers of the state as being "Lord of the Gate whence came all the diamonds." The word Gate here probably refers to Gutti, the hill-fort northeast of the old Vajrakarur (which in Telugu means village of diamonds) diamond mines in what is today the district of Kurnool. Some decades after Nunes and Paes, another Portuguese, this time a physician and naturalist named Garcia da Horta, lived in Goa on the west coast of India. He wrote following a trip to the high plateau of the Deccan in 1565, "Here the diamond is regarded as the king of precious stones," contrasting it with the pre-eminence of emerald and ruby in his native Europe. Perhaps of all his remarks, the most interesting concerns the then widespread belief that new diamonds were constantly being formed in rocks that had already been worked. Garcia da Horta claims, "When the galleries, which are made as high as a man can work, appear used up, they are abandoned, but they are reopened thirty or forty years later, for in that interval new diamonds are formed." This is not simply baseless fable or legend; it is an essentially accurate description of a particular method of operation. Although it is unlikely that anyone was aware of how it worked, this process exploited the effects of natural erosion, or the weathering of the rock on the site. In river or alluvial deposits the gravel or soil merely has to be washed in a sieve or a trough, but primary ore has to be crushed. When processing methods were primitive, as they were everywhere until the middle of the nineteenth century, they were profitable only when a large mass of the ore was attacked. This inevitably meant large losses, as all the diamonds in the rock could not be recovered at the first attempt. Consequently, the work site was abandoned for a time. The "rest period" allowed natural erosion to do its work and complete the breaking down of the ore—as was done in the early days in the South African diamond fields. When the debris was washed away some years later, more diamonds were recovered. This operation could be repeated successfully several times after varying intervals until the mine was completely empty. Before the natural process was understood, it was easy to assume that new diamonds were formed within the rock.

Garcia da Horta's information reveals that as early as the 16th century, diamond extraction in India was not limited to the relatively simple work on the alluvial deposits but was also concentrated on the bedrock, not only on the surface but underground as well. Hence the necessity of digging pits or galleries. The Dutch East India man Jan Huyghen van Linschoten was in Goa in 1595. Speaking of the mines he says, "They [diamonds] grow in the country of Deccan behind Ballagate [Balaghat], by the towns of Bisnagar [Vijayanagara], wherein are two or three hills, from whence they are digged. Whereof the King of Bisnagar doth reape great profitte; for he causeth them to be straightly watched, and hath farmed them out with this condition, that all diamonds above twenty mangellins in weight are for the King himselfe... There is yet another hill in the country of Deccan, which is called Velha, that is the old Rocke, from whence come the best diamonds and are sold for great price... Sometimes they find diamonds of one hundred and two hundred mangellins and more, but very few." He also observed that rough diamonds were brought from all parts of India to be sold to the Portuguese.

The reports by Marco Polo, Niccolo de Conti, Fernao Nunes, Domingos Paes, and Jan Huyghen van Linschoten are supplemented by a number of others. Unfortunately none of them had actually visited any of the working mines. All of them were speaking from second-hand sources, with varying degrees of accuracy. The questions then arise of where exactly the diamond mines were geographically located, who owned them, what was the mining procedure, where were the diamonds polished and faceted, what quantities of diamonds were extracted and what happened to the mines.

A series of pre-Cambrian rocks occur in the Deccan known locally as the Kurnool formation after the town of Kurnool where they were first studied by Dr. W. King, a geologist of the British Indian government. The rocks are divided into four strata, and the lowest of all is called the Banganapally Sandstones Group. The diamonds were found in the lowest stratum named after the minor Muslim principality in which they were studied.

Geographically, the diamond mines were located in the area that lies between the 13° 20' 17N latitude, and between 77° 80' 15E longitude, comprising an area about 210 miles long by 95 miles wide. Diamond deposits were located in three major geological settings whose politico-administrative geography kept changing. The settings are:

1. The Cuddapah group of diamond deposits on the Pennar River, comprising the deposits in the catchment area of the Pennar, which rises in the highlands of Mysore and reaches the Bay of Bengal north of Madras; from Cuddapah they extend about 60 miles up river. They are also called the Jennoor mines after a village near Cuddapah. The group also includes the deposits near Bellary on the lower Hagari, a tributary of the Tungabhadra.

2. The Nandyal group of diamond deposits between the Pennar and the Krishna near Banganapally, with the deposits around Nandyal,

Banganapally, Ramallakota and Kurnool, also known as the Kurnool mines, situated roughly between the Pennar and the junction of the Tungabhadra and the Krishna.

3. The Elluru group of diamond deposits on the lower Krishna, named after the town of Elluru, situated halfway between the mouths of the Krishna and the Godavari rivers about 45 miles inland from the Bay of Bengal. This is also called the Golconda group, and the famous mines of Kollur and Partiyala are located here.

This area now forms parts of the Krishna, Kurnool, Anantapur, and Cuddapah districts of Andhra Pradesh, and Bellary district in Karnataka. At various points in history, these were included in the territories of the Vijayanagara rajas, and the Bahmani, Qutb Shahi, and Adil Shahi sultans. At the fall of the Golconda dynasty in 1687, the area became part of the Mogul province of the Deccan, and with the emergence of the Nizams in 1720s, it came under the control of Hyderabad state. In 1766, the Nizam was forced to cede a large chunk of his territory called the Northern Circars in which the mines were located. But the Nizam wisely insisted on excluding the mine areas from the cession. Nearly two centuries later, the modern Indian states' reorganization resulted in the merger of Telugu-speaking areas into one state called Andhra Pradesh.

In all there were nearly 30 mines in operation between the 16th through the mid 19th centuries. We will go into the account of six major mines: Kollur, Partiyala, Gollapally, Mallavally, Ramallakota, and Banganapally. The focus will be on various aspects of mining such as the physical description of the mine, mining methods, state control, social composition of the labour force, and the wages paid to them. Some attention will be paid to the diamond traders and the overall impact of the trade on society. The account will end with a discussion on the decline of diamond mining.

Firsthand Accounts of the Mines

The most authentic and firsthand source of information about the mines comes from a Qutb Shahi revenue document in Persian. The document dated 1663 explicitly states that Musa Mahaldar gave 3500 *hun* (gold coin) to Qutb al-Mulk for the rent of *gani* (Telugu word for mine) Kollur. Further confirmation of this document comes from Persian records compiled during the Asaf Jahi Nizams' period in the 18th century. In the meanwhile, a number of European gem dealers and travellers actually journeyed to the mines. The first visitor (so far known) to the mines was the Flemish Jacques de Couttre who travelled from Goa to the Bijapur mines of Ramallakota in 1612. The Flemish traveller wrote a travelogue entitled *Andanzas asiaticas* or Journeys to Asia. The travelogue and its rich contents came to the attention of scholars only in the 1970s and the

1980s. In its detailed description of the mines, Couttre's book excels even Tavernier's in some respects.

The second traveller was an Englishman named William Methwold (1590-1652). Methwold, (also spelled Methold) was born in London and apprenticed at an early age to a merchant in Middleborough. He was on his own petition admitted into the East India Company's service in 1615, and sailed for Surat. Methwold travelled a great deal in India. On the way to the Deccan he missed the chilled spirits of his native land as did other Europeans in India's hot, humid climate. Many resorted to whatever liquors were available; in the Golconda area this happened to be the ever-present toddy. In memory of the delights of that infamous liquor, Methwold penned the following couplet:

The English and Dutch were Here
And drank toddy for want of Beer!

Accompanied by a fellow Englishman and Andries Soury, the Governor of Dutch Factories in Masulipatnam, Methwold visited the diamond mines of Golconda in 1622. Upon his return to England the narrative of his travels, entitled *Relations of the Kingdom of Golconda and Other Neighbouring Nations*, was published in 1626, in the fifth volume of Samuel Purchas's *Pilgrims*.

Methwold's visit was followed by that of the renowned French diamond merchant and seasoned traveler, Jean-Baptiste Tavernier (1605-89). Encouraged by Cardinal Jules Mazarin and later by King Louis XIV, Tavernier made several voyages to India. He left an account rich in valuable information, in the two-volume *Voyages*. He visited the three major mines of Kollur, Ramallakota, and Sambalpur, the last one in Orissa. The purpose of the visit according to him was "the diamond is the most precious of all stones, and it is the article of trade to which I am most devoted. In order to acquire a thorough knowledge of it, I resolved to visit all the mines, and one of the two rivers where diamonds were found; and as the fear of dangers has never restrained me in any of my journeys, the

Jean-Baptiste Tavernier, the French diamond merchant in oriental attire. Engraving from his book *Six Voyages* published in 1679. Bilbiothèque Nationale, Paris

terrible picture that was drawn of these mines, situated in barbarous countries to which one could not travel except by the most dangerous routes, served neither to terrify me nor to turn me from my intention. I have accordingly been at four mines..." He brought back enough jewels to win a baronetcy from the French king. In January 1640, some 18 years after Methwold's visit, Tavernier visited the three famous Golconda mines.

Visitors and Explorers to the Golconda Diamond Mine

	Name	Mine(s) Visited	Year(s)
1.	Jacques de Couttre	Ramallakota, Nandyal	1612
2.	William Methwold	Kollur, Mallavally, Vajrakarur	1622
3.	Jean-Baptiste Tavernier	Kollur, Vajrakarur	1640, 1645, 1653
4.	Henry Howard	Vajrakanur	1670's
5.	Streynsham Master	Gollapally	1679
6.	Benjamin Heyne	Mallavally	1795
7.	James Anderson	Mallavally	1820
8.	H. W. Voysey	Vajrakarur	1821
9.	W. Scott	Partiyala	1823
10.	T. J. Newbold	Vajrakarur, Ramallakota	1836, 1843, 1847
11.	Alexander Walker	Partiyala	1850

Visitors to the Diamond Mines

Some two decades after Tavernier's visit, the diamond mines were reported in a long memorandum written by Pieter de Lange, the Dutch ambassador at the Qutb Shahi court in Golconda who was incidentally a professional surgeon. According to Tavernier, a Golconda prince "suffered from a chronic pain in the head, and the physicians had ordered him to be bled under the tongue in four places; but he could not find any one willing to undertake it—because, as for surgery, the people of the country understand nothing about it." So the prince turned to Pieter de Lange. He was asked whether he could bleed well, to which he replied that "it was the least difficult operation in surgery." Soon after the Dutch surgeon was summoned to the royal palace and told that the prince wished to be bled on the following day in four places under the tongue, as his physicians had directed, but that he should take care not to draw more than eight ounces. He bled the prince in four places as directed under the tongue. On weighing the blood, he found that he had drawn eight ounces exactly! Pieter de Lange was, therefore, successful under conditions somewhat similar to those from which Shylock recoiled. Naturally, the Dutch surgeon earned the gratitude of the Golconda monarch by flawlessly performing delicate surgery on a long-suffering family member. Presumably Pieter de

Lange was provided every facility by the state officials on his trip to the mines. On 31 July 1663, he sent a report to the Dutch authorities in Batavia (the Dutch name for the present day Jakarta, Indonesia, where the headquarters of the Dutch East India Company was located), mentioning in addition to Ramallakota and Kollur, a place called Eragondapalam, near Gandikota.

Ten years after Pieter de Lange's report in 1677, the Royal Society in London received a report from the Right Honourable Earl Marshal, then Henry Howard (1628-1684), afterwards the sixth Duke of Norfolk. The report pertained to the diamond mines in the kingdoms of Golconda and Bijapur. It was published under the title "A Description of the Diamond Mines," in the journal called "Philosophical Transactions" June 25, 1677. Based on circumstantial evidence some historians attributed the authorship of the report to Nathaniel Cholmley, an East India Company factor. Apparently, Nathaniel Cholmley lived for many years at Golconda, and prior to 1679 was engaged in purchasing diamonds for his Company.

In the same decade of the 1670s, we find the next visitor to the Golconda mines, Sir Streynsham Master. Master (1640-1724) was the President of Council at Fort St. George. Fort. St. George refers to the East India Company's establishment in Madras, which was run by a council headed by a president, who was the chief executive officer. Streynsham Master presided over this council from January 1678 to July 1681. Between April 20-23, 1679, Master visited the Gollapally diamond mines, and reported his findings in a diary that was published later.

When did the mining begin? What did the mines look like? What were the mining methods and procedure in actual operation? In what manner did the state control and regulate the mining? Who were the miners and what was the social composition of the labour? What wages were paid to them? Who were the diamond traders? What impact did the diamond trade have on the economy of the Qutb Shahi kingdom and its successors? When and how did diamond mining end? To these questions we now turn.

The Mines

Diamond mines took different forms at different locations. The mine could be a tunnel, an open pit or a group of pits. The mines were dug in an area known to contain diamonds. Although the mines were mentioned in folklore and travelogues, no one dated their existence before Tavernier in 1645. According to the French traveller, who based his information on the authority of the natives, "the mines were discovered about two hundred years ago," that is around 1445. At Ramallakota, 18 miles west of Kurnool, he saw the mines, "All around the place where the diamonds are found the soil is sandy, and full of rocks and jungle, somewhat comparable to the neighbourhood of Fontainebleau. There in these rocks many veins, some of half a finger and some of a whole finger in width [are found]." Before Tavernier in 1612, Jacques de Couttre described the mines at Poli in the following manner as translated and paraphrased by a modern writer: "Poli was an underground mine two arquebus shots beneath the surface, along a rough and narrow passage, opening into a chamber big enough for a thousand men. Undergound temperatures were high, perhaps from the heat of the torches and lack of adequate air movement; the miners worked naked and covered with mud. They searched for diamonds in clay, the colour of steel." Couttre came out wet, covered with the clay and bearing a stone of 30 carats he had clandestinely purchased from a digger for 700 pagodas. This was, however, discovered and Couttre had to give it back, though his purchase price was restored and he incurred no further penalties. The poor digger was beaten to death, and according to the rules, Couttre could have suffered the same fate.

Centuries later, in January 1821 the professional geologist H. W. Voysey, visited the Banganapally mines not too far from Ramallakota. As would be expected, his report is laced with scientific terminology. He relates that the diamond-bearing formation was a "sandstone breccia," composed of a mixture of red and yellow jasper, chalcedony and hornstone, cemented by "quartz of the lava, the secondary minerals heliotrope and other chalcedony, opal, carbonate of lime (calcite) and zeolites".

Henry Howard's report about the mine of Vajrakarur in the neighbourhood of Banganapally, says that the "soil there is reddish." About the Kollur mine, the report says "the earth of the mine was yellowish." In it the diamonds were found "in great quantities in the vein, not lying in continued clusters" but "frequently so very scattered ... some time in the space of 1/4 of an acre ground was dug between two or three fathoms deep" yet " nothing was found." The mines that afford great stone usually lie "near the superficies of the earth... about three fathoms deep." The miners did not dig deeper as water would surface. Small diamonds were found at other places, where the earth was mixed with rugged stones. Sir Streynsham Master who saw the Gollapally mines described the ground as "loose, of a red fat sand and gravel, [filled] with great and small, black, red and white stone." On 25 May 1795, Benjamin Heyne visited Mallavally, which is in the Partiyala group of mines. According to Heyne, "all the different places in which the diamond has been hitherto found consists either in alluvial soil or in rocks of the latest formation, and containing such a great proportion of rounded pebbles as to have rather the appearance of a conglomerate than any other species of stone. The diamonds are not scattered through the whole of the beds from the surface in the diamond mines to the greatest depth hitherto dug; but confined to a single bed, always harder than the rest of the accompanying beds, and usually not exceeding a foot or two in thickness. The structure of all the places in which diamonds occur being similar, it will be sufficient to give an account of the beds found in these mines at Cuddapah, which I examined with as much care as possible."

"The uppermost, or superficial stratum, consists of sand, gravel, mixed with a small proportion of loam. Its thickness scarcely exceeds a foot and a half. Immediately under it is a bed of stiff bluish or black mud, similar to what we see in places that have inundated. It is about four feet thick, and contains no stones. The diamond bed comes next, and is easily distinguished from the incumbent bed, by the great number of large rounded stones which it contains. It is about two feet, or two and a half thick, and composed of large round stones, pebbles, and gravel, cemented together by clay."

Mining Methods

The most detailed accounts of diamond mining methods are given in Henry Howard's report, as well as in the observations of Pieter de Lange and Benjamin Heyne. As Methwold commented, mining was not carried out underground supported with timber, as in Europe, but in open pits... The earth was moved manually using the relay system, which was the reason why so many workers were employed. Success in finding diamonds depended on the skill of the miners who could judge after a little digging according to the soil, whether diamonds were going to be found in a particular area. In general, mines were a few feet deep. These pits were essentially excavated through three or four layers of earth, the men digging with crowbars and the women and children removing the earth. Soon the pit was at least 10 to 12 feet deep. The fifth layer was 3 to 4 feet thick and contained a large percentage of yellowish clay. The earth in this stratum was always moist with many rounded stones. These were called the matrix of the diamonds by the miners because, in general, the diamonds were found in these stones. Earth from this stratum was brought up to the surface to areas (or cisterns) which had been partitioned off, and the earth washed off with water, leaving behind the stones, though water often had to be brought in from quite far away, as far as one mile, and carried in headloads. The washed stones were then spread out to dry in another area, and the miners would examine them in sunlight, and the whitish clear stones were picked out. Usually the miners received additional payment as a bonus when they found diamonds, especially larger stones. An eyewitness account of how the cisterns were made and later used to find the stones is given by Howard:

"When they start mining near the place where they dig, they raise a wall with such rugged stones as they find at hand of about two feet high and six feet over, flooring it with the same; for the laying of which they have no other mortar than earth tempered with water. To strengthen and make it

Top
Diamond washing in Ramallakota mine.
(Source unknown)

Above
Digging of diamonds in Ramallakota mine.
(Source unknown)

tight, they throw up a bank against the side of it. In one bank, they leave a small vent about two inches from the bottom by which it empties itself into a little pit, made in the earth to receive small stones, if by chance they should run through. The vent being stopped, they fill the cistern they have made with water, soaking therein as much of the earth they dig out of the mines, as it can conveniently receive at a time, breaking the clods, picking out the great stones and stirring it with shovels, till the water is all muddy; the gravelly stuff falling to the bottom; then they open the vent, letting out the foul water and supplying it with clean water, till all the earthy substance be washed away, and none but a gravely remains at the bottom. They never examine the stuff they have washed away except between the hours of ten and three lest any cloud by interposing intercept the brisk beam of the sun, which they hold very necessary to assist them in their search of the diamonds."

The Mining Labour

The labour that worked on these mines included men and women children aged 10-12. According to Howard, they were all "ethnicks", i.e. Telugu-speaking "natives", not Mussalmans. As for the type of labour force, "some experts were employed for searching" the diamonds, while others did the more routine manual labour. Their employees had to sit nearby and watch them closely as they could part with precious discoveries. On finding a large stone, many tried to hide it in order to sell the find privately. Each mining location provided employment for 30,000 to 60,000 workers every day. Mining labour was constantly shifted around by the employers to prevent the labourers from acquiring detailed knowledge of where diamonds could be found. No wonder that modern visitors to old mines cannot find people whose ancestors may have been there.

The Diamond Trade, Merchants and Speculators

Diamonds had, from time immemorial, played an important part in India's trade with Asia and Europe. Golconda was no doubt the world's largest producer of diamonds between the sixteenth and early eighteenth centuries. The only other place in the world that yielded diamonds in any quantity was Borneo, where the production was small and access difficult. For the European who traded in the precious stones, there was general agreement that there was no safer or surer way of remitting one's gain, especially one's ill-gotten gains, to Europe than the transport of diamonds, either concealed in one's own person or locked in a sea captain's strong box. Stitched into an armpit seam or a leg of baggy trousers, diamonds and pearls or rubies were inconspicuous to port authorities who might otherwise be tempted to impose heavy taxes on such wealth. In short, the diamonds served the same purpose as does paper currency, bank cheques, or a credit card today. Demand always exceeded supply and diamonds were more costly within India than overseas. The success of the diamond trade between India and Europe depended to a great extent on keeping Indians in ignorance of the price that the stones fetched on the Continent and on maintaining secrecy in Europe about the prices at which they had been bought in Golconda. As soon as Golconda merchants found out about the prices for their stones in Europe they demanded much more in selling prices, for the merchants themselves had to pay no small rents for acquiring diamonds.

At each mine or a cluster of mines, a licensee, usually a Telugu Brahmin, paid a set amount to control all mining and supply concessions at the workings. The mine controller also turned over all diamonds found over a certain size to the Qutb Shahi or Adil Shahi royal treasury. Usually this meant all large stone bigger than 10-13 carats. The royal prerogative was strictly enforced as gleaned from a Dutch report of 1643 - 44. The Dutch officials reported bitterly that they had been forced by Mir Jumla, a Golconda officer, to return a stone of 17.75 *manjali* which had been bought at a very reasonable price for them by the Masulipatanm merchants, since all big stones belonged to the king. The prerogative continued to be exercised even at the close of the eighteenth century, and all stones which weighed more than one pagoda (European word for hun, a gold coin, not to be confused with the same word for temple) belonged to the Nizam of Hyderabad, even though this norm was of little real value since no big stones were being found by then.

Diamond mines were also farmed out by the Sultan to officials who bid for this right, and provided steady revenue for the state, estimated at 300, 00 pagodas annually by Joannes de Laet though this information may be a little suspect. The Dutch official Pieter de Lange in his exhaustive report of 1663 mentioned that the annual revenue to the king from the Kollur mines ten years earlier had ranged from 100,000 to 130,000 or 150,000 pagodas. But recent disturbances and the "bad government" and tyranny of Governor Jamal Baig had resulted in the local people running away. An official named Bhimaji Brahmanna, the lessee of the mines, had sent only 10,000 pagodas that year because he was not committed to any fixed sum, though he had obtained the lease for 20,000 pagodas. This concession was intended to give a boost to the industry and revive it locally. Streynsham Master estimated that the mining rights of the Gollapally mines had been farmed for 60,000 pagodas. Based on this calculation, de Laet's overall total of 300,00 pagodas as the sultan's revenue from all diamond mines seems reasonable.

Merchants who wanted to prospect for diamonds rented a selected plot of land from the revenue farmers. Besides rent, an additional payment was made depending on the number of miners employed. A further source of revenue for the farmer was the customs duties charged on all incoming goods. If for any reason private investors did not come forward to lease land for mining, the mines could be operated by the sultan himself. This was the case with the Golconda sultan as reported by de Lange in the seventeenth century, and the Nizam in the eighteenth century as noted by Heyne.

De Lange observed a variant of the system which was followed in Kollur. There anybody who wished to "seek his fortune under this hard rock and earth" applied to the Qutb Shahi governor for permission to work a plot of land, and for as many workers as he wished. In the 1650s, the governor was paid two pagodas per day per worker, but the latter had been paid so little and treated so miserably that most ran away resulting in a decline in diamond revenues to the sultan. Measures were instituted to improve the situation, including a payment to the governor, of seven pagodas per month for ten workers of which he kept two while distributing the rest to the labourers.

It is difficult to hazard more than an inference at the initial investment required for diamond mining. From the figures given by Master, for one month the merchants needed to lay out three to five pagodas in rent, an additional three pagodas as payment to the governor for 40 workers, and 50 pagodas as wages. Over and above this, the investor had to pay for wages of supervisors, provisions at inflated prices, and the duties on incoming goods. Since there was no guarantee that diamonds would be found at fixed or regular intervals, the merchant had to be prepared to continue his investment indefinitely. In the long run the investor seldom lost, as illustrated in the case of a Portuguese merchant cited by Howard. Evidently, around 1610, a Portuguese gentleman went to Vajrakarur and spent a large sum of money, around 100,000 pagodas, in search of diamonds, without success. He then sold everything he had with him, even his last pair of clothes. On the last day, when he could still pay the wages of the labourers, he prepared a cup of poison which he intended to drink that night if no diamonds were found. In the evening, a fine stone of 26 pagodas' weight was brought to him by the workers. He took the stone with him to Goa, and to commemorate its discovery, he put up a stone tablet on which the following doggerel was engraved in Telugu:

Your wife and children sell, sell what you have,
Spare not your clothes, nay, make yourself a slave,
But money get, then to Karur make haste,
There search the mines, a prize you'll find at last.

The diamond merchants were banias of Gujarat who for generations had left their country to take up this trade in which they had such success that it was now completely monopolized by them. They supplied diamonds to merchants in the capital Golconda (and later Hyderabad), Bijapur, Surat,

Agra, and Delhi. In general, all first sales of diamonds took place at the mines against cash payment on the spot. Golconda and Hyderabad were the chief markets of the diamonds.

It is hard to estimate the average annual output of diamonds in value or weight. From the comments made from time to time by the Dutch factors on the Coromandel coast, it is evident that there were wide fluctuations in the supply of diamonds, since digging often stopped due to wars and severe weather. The prices tended to fluctuate due to erratic supply and high demand. There seems to be no doubt that throughout the seventeenth century the demand for diamonds far exceeded supply. According to de Lange, rough diamonds yielded 118 percent profit in the Netherlands. From October 1662 to March 1663, diamonds worth 191,000 pagodas had been sent from the Kollur mine to various stations: Surat received 80,000 pagodas, followed by Goa 70,000; Madras 23,000; and Masulipatnam 18,000. None of the stones were returned as unsaleable. Staggeringly, an equal value of diamonds were sold at Golconda. De Lange's report also mentions "Bania caravans, which bought up diamonds worth 100,000 pagodas in a single trip."

The Diamond Industry's Impact on the Economy and Society

It is clear that diamond mining, though a highly restricted and localized activity, became an important part of the economy. It undoubtedly helped the growth of regional and long-distance trade, especially with Persia and other areas in the Middle East. Famed merchants arrived in Golconda from renowned centres of carpet-making such as Bukhara, Shiraz, Isfahan, Kashan, and Mashhad. The wealth acquired by the nobles through the diamond trade went into the construction of impressive mansions lavishly decorated with the finest Kashani mosaic tiles and furnished with the choicest Persian carpets. The descendants of the carpet-makers continue to be active in the profession in our own time in several towns of Andhra Pradesh.

Hyderabad, the Golconda sultanate's newly-laid-out capital, grew rapidly in settlement area and population to become the dominant centre of consumption in the region. Moreover, the presence of the Qutb Shahi court stimulated the evolution of Hyderabad as the major market for large-scale mercantile and state finance in the Deccan. The city's location on the main commercial route between the west coast ports and those of the east coast also ensured that it would become an important entrepot for inland trade in the Deccan. Two hundred miles to the east, Masulipatnam, possessing an excellent anchorage, came to rival the great Mogul port of Surat in Gujarat, in the size of its international trade.

The City of Masulipatnam. Etching and line-engraving. Source: Peter Baldaeus, *A True and Exact Description of the Most Celebrated East India Coasts of Malabar and Coromandel*, London, 1703

Diamond mining was naturally affected by the politico-military events involving the region. On several occasions during the seventeenth century, military conflict between Golconda and the Moguls led to mine closures, in addition to work stoppages due to labour disputes. The major disruption came towards the close of the 17th century. After a protracted siege of nine months, the last Qutb Shahi sultan Abul Hasan Tana Shah surrendered to the forces of Mogul Emperor Aurangzeb in 1687 as the Adil Shahi sultan had a done year earlier in neighbouring Bijapur. The territories of the two kingdoms were now ruled by a Mogul *subahdar* or governor. The large-scale fighting severely damaged the mining operations, and the mines remained idle for quite some time.

The diamond mines of Golconda and Bijapur were one of the richest prizes to be won in the Deccan. It is a measure of the difficulties the Moguls faced in the newly-conquered provinces that it took several years before the mining resumed. As late as mid-1692 François Martin, the French governor of Pondicherry noted that diamond mining and trading had completely ceased. Money formerly invested in that trade was now put to other uses. Finally, in the same year, Emperor Aurangzeb approved new administrative arrangements for the nearly defunct mines. The mines in Bijapur were to come under the supervision of the *faujdar* of Kurnool; those north of the Krishna river were to come under the *faujdar* of Khammamet, Hasan Quli Khan; and those to the south of the Krishna river were to come under Ali

Mardan Khan, *faujdar* of Hyderabad Karnataka. These officers were to put the mines on a paying basis; the few mines which had been working did not produce enough to pay the salaries of the administrative staff.

The revived operation of the mines, now under the direct supervision of Mogul accountants employed by the *khalisa*, revenue department was similar to arrangements in effect under Golconda. Private entrepreneurs paid a fixed fee for the exclusive right to mine a measured land for diamonds. The mining contractors hired labourers to do the actual work. Profits came from the right to keep all stones below a certain size. All diamonds heavier than the weight of a gold *hun* (three-eighths of an ounce, according to Niccolao Manucci) became the property of the Mogul emperor. Predictably, those mining contractors or miners who found large stones, and who could evade the imperial authorities, took the risk of smuggling their finds out of the mines and selling them in the open market. Still, smuggling was not always possible in the crowded conditions of the mines. More often, the discovery of a large stone was a public event which was immediately reported to the emperor by the provincial newswriter.

In the second half of 1692, the mines began steady and profitable production once again. Shipments of the largest and best stones, sometimes as many as eighteen at a time, travelled from the mines to the Emperor's camp in the western Deccan. Simultaneously, a significant alteration occurred in the pattern of the diamond trade. Diamond merchants, agents, buyers, and speculators no longer frequented the great diamond quarter of Golconda, the Caravan-i Sahu, which under the Qutb Shahis had been the busiest diamond market in the world. Instead, the trade focussed on the vast assemblage of Aurangzeb's camp where, in the dry season, stones, money, and a market among the Mogul nobility could be found. Another subsidiary market was in Madras on the southern coast.

However, there were now new problems of security in the production and transport of diamonds. For the first time the diamond mines were walled around and garrisoned to defend them against raiders— a measure of the new political instability of the Deccan. There was also a distinct possibility that large diamonds sent from the mines would never reach the emperor. Thus, in 1702, officials at the mines reported the find of a stone of spectacular size weighing 2 1/4 ounces, which was seized by the Maratha freebooters en route to the imperial camp. Still, despite these problems, the reopened diamond mines of Golconda and Bijapur provided highly negotiable and prestigious additions to the income of the imperial treasury in the last fifteen years of Aurangzeb's reign.

Aurangzeb's death in 1707 signalled the decline of the Mogul Empire. New powers emerged in different parts of the country. The Mogul rule in the Deccan was menaced by the Marathas in the western portion of the region. At length, Nizam al-Mulk Asaf Jah, a reputed Mogul noble, dissatisfied with the conditions of the Empire, declared his independence in Aurangabad in or around 1720 and founded the Nizam's Dominions. The Golconda and Bijapur territories naturally became part of the new dominion. No major disruption in mining was reported due to the political changes at higher levels in Aurangabad and Delhi. Due to the political and military pressure, the Nizam of Hyderabad was forced to cede the Northern Circars to the East India Company in 1766. But the Nizam made sure that the Partiyala group of diamond mines located in the Circars were exempt from cession, and remained as Hyderabad enclaves in the East India Company's domains. In 1795, Dr. Benjamin Heyne, an Englishman visited the mines at Mallavally and filed a detailed report to the President in Council at Fort St. George. He reported that this particular mine was still active, contrary to popular belief that mining was a thing of the past. He was of the opinion that the diamond strata were not nearly exhausted, being intact and close to the pits whence famous stones had been taken.

Nothing more is heard of the diamond mines until we hear of H.W. Voysey's trip to the diamond mines of Banganapally in Kurnool. Voysey (1791-1824), the first professional geologist of the East India Company, visited the diamond mines at Banganapally, some 40 miles southeast of Kurnool in January 1821. Since Voysey, a number of geologists such as T. J. Newbold (to Vajrakarur and Ramallakota in the 1830s and 1840s); James Anderson (Mallavally in 1820); and W. Scott (Partiyala in 1823), among others, employed by the East India Company visited old diamond workings. Each went away with the impression that although the mines looked exhausted, work should continue with better techniques and tools.

Shortly before his death in 1850 Alexander Walker, an East India Company official, saw only two mines being worked at Partiyala which were rented for a paltry sum of 8 annas (coins current in Hyderabad at the time) per month, one to a Mussalman, and the other to a Telingi. The diamonds found were very small, and if the searcher realised four or five rupees a month for his trouble he deemed himself fortunate. Walker further mentions the "numberless knolls and pits hollowed down to the underlying granite, fully attesting to the extent and strictness of the search..." He concluded that the tract was exhausted, and made the notable remark, "but this is scarcely probable, as the stratum extends under the villages where from superstitious motives it has not been touched." His remarks were echoed in 1876 by Richard Francis Burton (1840-1922), a Victorian traveller. Burton was an extremely unusual explorer, having travelled in disguise to Mecca and Medina, the two most holy places of Islam from which non-Muslims are barred. A polyglot, Burton had travelled to the Brazilian diamond mines. He has left behind a travelogue of high quality. His trip to Partiyala was motivated by a desire to get rich quick. After visiting the old mines, Burton concluded that diamond digging in the Nizam's Dominions had been prematurely abandoned. He attempted, by letters to the British press and in various reports, to enlist the interests of British capitalists. But it was all too vague for British businessmen, and none of them got into practical exploration. Failing to tempt the British financiers, Burton had long meetings with Nawab Salar Jang, the able *diwan* of Hyderabad state from 1853-83. Circumstances suggest that he may have urged the *diwan* to consider mining afresh, for we know that after years of neglect, an attempt to open the Partiyala mine was made by the Hyderabad Deccan Mining Company in 1890. The Company had obtained the mineral rights over this area. The actual pit in which the ancient miners had worked was attacked, and the excavated alluvial was washed by modern machinery resulting in the extraction of 3,444 stones weighing 2085 7/8 carats. Most of the diamonds

Partiyala diamond mine in Hyderabad State. Panel of a three-plate panoramic photograph by Raja Deen Dayal, 1885. © Omar Khalidi

were poor, many merely chips, probably the result of the pounding described by Tavernier. The project was stopped in 1894 due to poor returns.

Leonard Munn, a modern geologist, suggested that instead of attacking the ancient mines, it would have better to attack new ground overlooked by the old miners. He was proven right at least in one case. P. Orr & Sons of Madras discovered a large stone near Wajra Karur in the Kurnool area in the early 20th century. It was named Goor-di-Noor, and valued at 10,000 to 15, 000 pounds sterling.

Since the middle of the nineteenth century the devoted staff of the Geological Survey of India have done extensive exploration of the diamond mines using new techniques and modern equipment used by trained personnel. But extraction so far has not been successful. The mines now lie entirely idle. The villagers can be seen ploughing around the pebble-strewn edges of the pits which once disgorged such wonderful wealth. Press reports in the Indian media speak from time to time of the interest of foreign companies in the exploration of diamonds in Andhra Pradesh, but positive results have yet to occur.

The Famous Diamonds of Golconda

The Golconda diamonds were dispersed into the world as a result of legitimate trade, smuggling, theft, and other unlawful means. Today no individual, no museum, no jeweller in Hyderabad possesses diamonds of any historical value. So where are the Golconda diamonds now?

Despite his wish and many travels in India, Tavernier had not seen the Mogul crown jewels, most of which consisted of Golconda diamonds sent as tribute by the Qutb Shahi sultans. After several entreaties, in November 1665, Tavernier's dream came true when he was received at the Mogul court. Aurangzeb sat on one of the seven jewel-encrusted thrones and watched while four eunuchs brought in two large trays lacquered with gold leaf and covered with small cloths, one of gold-embroidered red velvet and one of green. As the emperor stood, two keepers of the jewels counted each stone three times and wrote out an inventory. This clearly took a maddeningly long time. Tavernier, commenting on this practice, remarks that "the Indians do everything with great care and composure, and when they see anyone acting in a hurry or irritated they stare at him in silence and laugh at him for being a fool."

After an agonizing wait, however, the head keeper placed the jewels in the French traveller's hand. The first was a giant diamond, a rose-cut piece later called The Great Mogul. In form, he said, it was like an egg cut in half. Many writers claim that The Great Mogul was cut into pieces of which the Koh-i-Noor is one. But the Koh-i-Noor's original lack of fire and shape make that unlikely. The Great Mogul simply vanished from the imperial treasury and has not been discovered to date. Many of the historic diamonds that Tavernier named have been the favourite tramping grounds for writers about diamonds for more than a century and what is truth and what fiction is now impossible to determine. This is clearly the case with the Koh-i-Noor and other diamonds originating in Nadir Shah's sack of Delhi.

Name	Colour	Shape	Weight (carats) Rough	Weight (carats) Cut	Last Reported Owner, Location
Agra	Light Pink	Modified Cushion	46	28.15	CIBA Corporation Hong Kong
Ahmedabad	Pink	Pear		15	Sold by Christie's Geneva, Nov. 15, 1995
Arcots (2 diamonds)		Pear		31.01	Sold by Harry Winston American client in 1995 and 1960
Black Orioff/Oriov	Gun Metal	Cushion	195	67.5	Sold by Sotheby in 1991
Conde	Pink	Pear		9.01	Chateau de Chantilly, France
Darya-i-Noor	Pale Pink	Rectagular Step cut		175-195	Bank-i-Markazi Tehran, Iran
Dresden Green	Fancy Green	Pear-shaped Brilliant cut		40.7	Green Vaults Dresden, Germany
Florentine	Light Yellow	Irregular, 9-sided double rose cut		137.27	Stolen in 1920 from the Imperial Family of Austria
Golconda	Yellow			30	Last owned in 1960 by Muriel Reynolds, wife of tobacco millionaire, R. J. Reynolds
Golconda d'Or	Yellow	Emerald cut	130	95.4	On permanent display at Dunkings, the jewellers, Melbourne, Australia until1980 when stolen
Golconda Graff		Brilliant cut		47.29	Graff Diamonds, Ltd., London purchased it in 1984
Great Mogul		Rose cut	787.5	186	
Great Table	Light Pink	Flat, Oblong	242.31	280	
Hastings				101	Presented to King Charles II of England by Warren Hastings in 1786 on behalf of Nizam Ali Khan. May have formed part of the Hanry Winston, NY
Hope	Grayish Blue	Cushion	112	45.5	Smithsonian Institution, Washington, D.C.
Hortensia	Pale Pink	Flat and Rectangular		20.53	Gallerie d'Apollo, Louvre Museum, France
Idol's Eye	Slight Bluish	Brilliant cut		70.21	Sold by Lawrence Graff of London in 1983
Kirti Noor	Pink	Pear		15	
Koh-i-Noor	White	Oval	279	105.6	Tower of London, England Crown Jewels of Great Britain
Nizam		Concave-based, elongated dome stone	340-400	277	In Hydrabad State Treasury in early 1850's
Noor-al-Ain	Rose Pink	Oval drop		60 est.	Bank-i-Markazi, Tehran, Iran
Orioff/Oriov	Slightly tinted white	Half and egg, rose cut above, flat E' unfaceted below		189.6	State Armoury Museum, Kremlin, Moscow, Russia
Pigot (t)		Oval cut	45-85		Albanian Gen. Ali Pasha had the diamond crushed to pieces before his death in 1822
Regent/Pitt	White with Blue tinge	Mogul cut	410	140.5	Gallerie d'Apollo, Louvre Museum, France
Sancy		Pear, double rose cut, rose cut, rectangular E' pentagonal facets		55.23	Gallerie d'Apollo, Louvre Museum, France
Shah	Light Yellow	Bar-shaped		189.6	State Armoury Museum, Kremlin, Moscow, Russia
Shah Japan	Pale Pink	Table cut of octagonal outline		56.71	Was on sale at Christie's Geneva, in 1985.
Taj-i-Mah	White	Mogul cut	115.06		Bank-i-Markazi, Tehran, Iran
Jacob (a South African diamond)	White		184.75		Reserve Bank of India, New Delhi, India
Wittlesbach	Blue	Oval		35.5	Acquired by a private collection in 1964 from Joseph Komkommer, a Belgian diamond dealer

The diagrams contain labels:

A — The Thickness. The upper Part. the under Part. 112 ½ Caratts.

The Top. The Bottome. 51 9/16 Ca. ½ Thickness.

31 ⅜ Ca. the Thickness. The Top.

the Topp. ½ Thickness. 29 ½ C.

D — ½ upper Part. ½ Bottome. 20 1/10 Ca.

20 ¼ Ca. the Top. ½ Bottome.

16 ¼ Cas. 13 9/16 Cas.

16 1/16 Cas. ½ Topp. ½ Thickness.

B — 14 ⅜ C. ½ Lower part. the topp.

th. Bottome. the Topp. 13 ⅝ Ca.

½ Topp. ½ Thickness. 10 ¼ Ca.

9 Car. 33 Car.

C — 20 5/6 Car. ½ Bottome. ½ Top.

7 Car. 5 Ca.

10 11/10 Ca. 32 Cas. 24 ⅞.

1. 2. 3.

Ħ.1. Ħ.2. Ħ.3. Ħ.4. Ħ.5. Ħ.6. Ħ.7. Ħ.8.

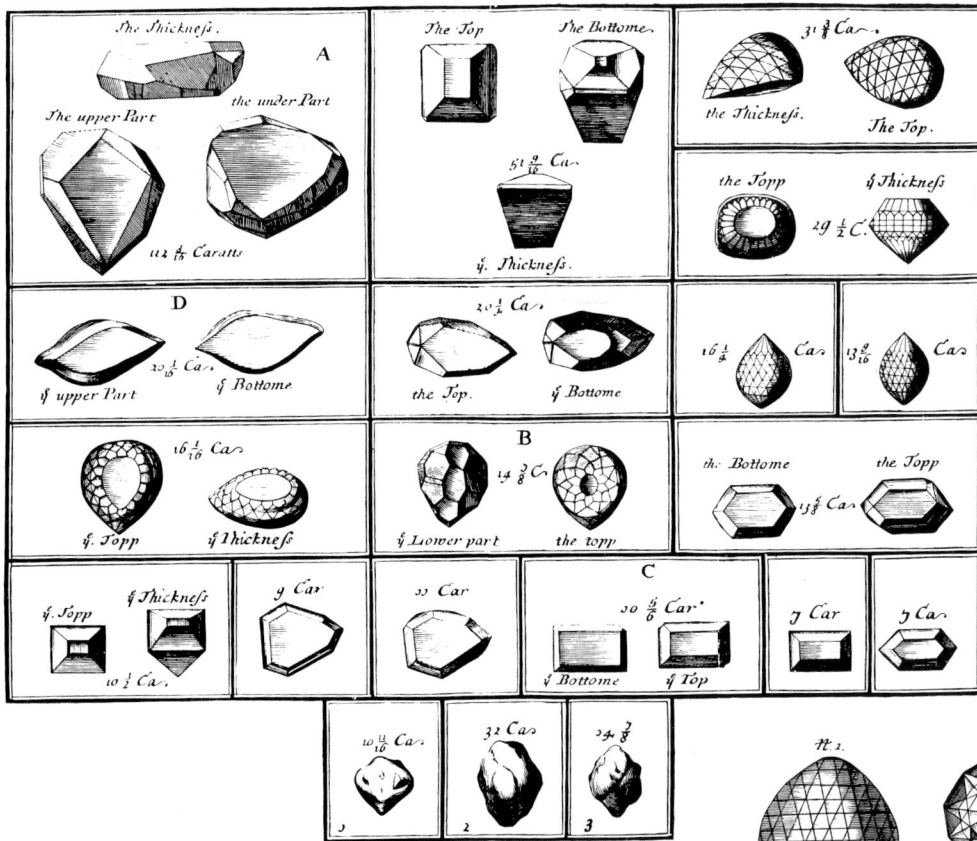

Above
Tavernier's diamond illustrations (a). Diamond A, top left is the violet-blue diamond from which the Hope was cut. Jean-Baptiste Tavernier's *Six Voyages*. Bibliothèque Nationale, Paris

Right
Tavernier's diamond illustrations (b) No.1 is the almost 280-carat stone which belonged to Aurangzeb, known as the Great Mogul, from which the Koh-i-Noor was cut. No. 2 is probably the Florentine; Tavernier calls it a citron-coloured diamond and said it belonged to the Grand Duke of Tuscany. No.3 is a 242-carat stone which was named as the Great Table. No. 4 was a diamond Tavernier bought for a friend. No. 5 is the same as no. 4 after being recut in Europe. No. 6 is a diamond from the famous Kollur mine. Nos. 7 & 8 are the cleavages from a single stone Tavernier brought from Golconda and had cut in Europe. The exact whereabouts of these diamonds are unknown except for the Koh-i-Noor

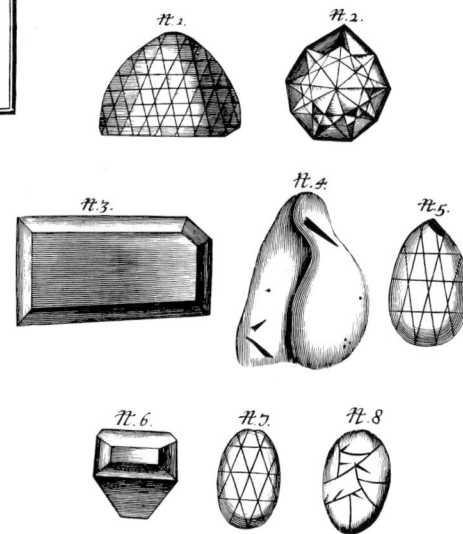

The Koh-i-Noor

Perhaps the most celebrated Indian diamond and the one best-known overseas, the Koh-i-Noor, or the mountain of light, has a colourful history. It is frequently cited in everyday conversation in the subcontinent as the most precious of things. Poets have rhymed and sung of its stunning brilliance and novelists have waxed eloquent of its fabulous value. It is a popular female name among Bengali Muslims. Indian and Pakistani politicians have demanded its return, while some demonstrated against Queen Elizabeth in October 1997 asking for the diamond's return to its rightful owners. If India was figuratively the brightest jewel in the British empire, the Koh-i-Noor is quite literally the most brilliant jewel in the imperial regalia. The Koh-i-Noor presents us with the greatest number of stories and novels in English since it came into the possession of Queen Victoria, who ruled England between 1837-1901, the Victorian era.

The Koh-i-Noor has the longest and the most controversial history for any extant diamond in the world. As related by Jean-Baptiste Tavernier, this diamond was found in Kollur about 1656-57 and was presented in an uncut form by Mir Jumla, the Golconda general, to Emperor Shah Jahan. The stone then weighed 900 *rattis* or 787 1/2 carats. In 1665, Tavernier handled this diamond in Aurangzeb's treasury; it then weighed 319 1/2 *rattis* or 279 carats. It had been reduced to this size by a Venetian imposter named Hortensio Borgio by wasteful grinding, instead of cleaving. Borgio barely escaped decapitation by paying a huge fine for his stupidity and lack of skill. Nothing was heard of the Koh-i-Noor for nearly a century until the invasion of Delhi by Nadir Shah, the Persian monarch. In 1739, Nadir Shah captured the Indian capital and the Mogul palace. For 58 days he and his soldiers carried out a brutal massacre, *qatl-i aam*. Indeed, the killing was on such a large scale that Asaf Jah Nizam al-Mulk, the Mogul noble and later, the founder of the Hyderabad state was compelled to tell the Persian invader that soon he would have to revive the dead population in order to continue the killing as few were left to die. Apart from the killing, the loot was enormous and included the famous Takht-i Tawus, or the Peacock Throne of enamelled gold adorned with several thousand precious stones, which the conqueror shipped to Persia. This throne is still part of the Iranian state treasure. Meanwhile, some of his soldiers systematically ransacked the Mogul palaces seeking, among other things, a famous diamond known throughout the world to be among the crown jewels. At last a woman among the conquered Mogul's harem betrayed the secret. The coveted jewel, she said, was hidden in the folds of the emperor's turban. It was not customary to attack the defeated kings personally, so Nadir Shah took advantage of an old oriental tradition and invited the emperor to a banquet celebrating the Persian victory. At dinner, he suggested politely that the two rulers, the victorious and the vanquished,

Oppsite Page
The Koh-i-Noor, detached from the Queen Mother's Crown, HMSO, London

exchange turbans. Even while speaking, he effected the change, removing first his own sheep-skin turban adorned with gems then removing the other's and shifting the latter swiftly to his own head. The defeated Mogul Emperor showed neither chagrin nor concern. Indeed, so unperturbed was he that Nadir Shah feared he had been duped. Hastily he withdrew to his tent and unrolled the silk to find a single great diamond. "Koh-i-Noor!" he murmured. "Mountain of light!" and so he named the stone. Thus the rare stone passed into the hands of a "rarer" king Nadir Shah, who took it to his native Persia.

A cruel and tyrannical ruler, Nadir Shah was assassinated less than a decade after possessing the diamond. From this time onwards, the Koh-i-Noor acquired a reputation for bringing bad luck to its possessor. Four kings succeeded to Nadir Shah's throne in as many years. The fourth one, Sayyid Muhammad, had his predecessor, Shahrukh Mirza, blinded and tortured in order to gain possession of the diamond, but his victim endured even the most excruciating punishments. In 1751, Ahmad Shah Durrani, who had seized the throne of nearby Afghanistan, decided to intervene in Persian affairs to restore order. He released Shahrukh Khan, who presented him with the splendid jewel as a token of thanks. About four decades later, in 1793, the stone fell into the hands of Zamanshah, Ahmad Shah Durrani's grandson. Dethroned by his brother, the cruel Shujaa Shah and then cast into prison, Zaman Shah refused to reveal what he had done

Below
Mogul Emperor Muhammad Shah dressed in a white *jama* in the company of Nadir Shah, the Persian invader, who forced him to part with the Koh-i-Noor in the sack of Delhi in 1739. Mogul miniature, Musèe Guimet, Paris

Opposite Page
Mir Jumla, the Golconda official and diamond merchant who presented the Koh-i-Noor to Shah Jahan in 1665. Deccani miniature. Bibliothèque Nationale, Paris

with the Koh-i-Noor and pressed it into the mud wall of his prison cell, where it was discovered by chance some years later. Shujaa wore it only a short time. Ousted by his nephew Mahmud, he was sent into exile and found refuge with the Sikh ruler Ranjit Singh, the "Lion of Punjab." Shujaa had somehow managed to keep the Koh-i-Noor, but was obliged by his host to "sell" it to him. When Ranjit Singh asked him the price of the stone, Shujaa haughtily replied, "Take five strong men. Let the first throw a stone northward, the second eastward, the third southward, the fourth westward, and the fifth upward, into the air. Fill all the space thus outlined with gold and you will still not have achieved the value of the Mountain of Light."

Ranjit Singh had the stone mounted with two others in a bracelet of enameled gold, which is now in the Tower of London. Cut in the old Indian manner, the Koh-i-Noor weighed 279 carats. It remained in the Lahore treasury until 1849. In that year, following the defeat of the Sikhs in the Second Sikh War, the Punjab was annexed by Britain, at that time still represented by the powerful East India Company. When the treasury of Lahore was seized in lieu of the government's outstanding debts to the Company, the Koh-i-Noor was presented to Queen Victoria in a formal levèe. The Mountain of Light left India in 1850 and has never returned. In 1851 it was displayed in the Crystal Palace during the Great Exhibition in London, but many visitors found it disappointing. Its Indian cut did not do it justice, and it hardly deserved its name. So the Queen decided to have it re-cut, and a famous diamond cutter named Voorsanger of the Coster Company was summoned from Amsterdam. Prince Albert, the Queen's husband, himself placed the gem on the 4 horse-power steam engine installed for this special purpose. In gaining the benefit of the brilliant oval cut it now has, the Koh-i-Noor was sharply reduced from 279 to 108.93 carats.

The Queen was superstitious and took seriously the old Indian legend that said the Koh-i-Noor would bring misfortune to men who possessed it, though not to women. Consequently, she specified in her will that when the diamond was inherited by a male sovereign, it should be worn only by his wife. Her request has always been scrupulously respected. Richard Burton, the famous Victorian traveller relates the interesting anecdote in Hyderabad about the belief in ill-luck associated with the diamond,

Above
The Koh-i-Noor on public view at the Crystal Palace Exposition in London in 1851. Most people were disappointed by it.
[Artist, source unknown]

Top
The Koh-i-Noor as it was set by the Persians.
[Artist, source unknown]

Opposite Page
The Queen Mother's crown contains the 188.93 carat : Koh-i-Noor diamond which is set on the cross resting on the circlet of the crown. HMSO, London

THE KOH-I-NOOR'S TRAVELS: WHO ACQUIRED IT, WHEN, HOW?			
INDIA	PERSIA	AFGHANISTAN	ENGLAND
Mir Jumla (ca. 1650, bought?)			
Shahjahan (gift, Mir Jumila, 8 July 1656)	Nadir Shah Afshar (1 May 1739, strategem, Mohammed Shah)		
Mohammed Shah "Rangila' (1719, Mughal legacy)		Ahmed Shah Adbali (17 June 1747, Nadir Shah's deathbed?)	
		Timur Shah (October 1777, legacy, father Ahmed Shah)	
Ranjit Singh (1 June 1813, ransom, Shah Shuja)			
		Shah Shuja (July 1803, conquest)	
The East India Company (April 1849, conquest)			Queen Victoria (3 July 1850, gift, Lord Dalhousie)

"When my friend...heard about the imminent departure of the diamond from India to Britain to be presented to the Queen, he spat upon the ground, and with an expression of horror uttered the usual Muslim exclamation under the circumstances, 'tobah!' repentance in the name of Allah! "Are they going to send that accursed thing to the Queen! May she refuse it! All natives spit with exclamation of horror whenever they hear it mentioned."

In 1937 the stone was placed in the crown of Queen Elizabeth (now known as the Queen Mother, not to be confused with Elizabeth II), wife of George VI. Since then the Queen Mother alone has worn it on occasions of high ceremony. Of all the precious stones among the British crown jewels in the Tower of London, the Koh-i-Noor is not the most exceptional— the Cullinan is much larger — but it is certainly the most famous, and the one with the longest history.

The Independence of India and Pakistan in August 1947 brought home the fact that a great deal of the subcontinent's cultural property had been taken to Britain. Naturally, nationalist sentiment demanded the return of all artifacts. But India's Minister for Education, the venerable Maulana Abulkalam Azad told the Indian Parliament in 1952 that his "government has not at any stage contemplated asking for the return of the Koh-i-Noor, as it is not an art object and now forms a part of the British crown jewels." Some two decades later, Pakistan's Prime Minister Zulfiqar Ali Bhutto, involved in a diplomatic row with Britain, demanded the diamond's return for, according to him, the stone had been taken away from Lahore, now a part of his country. The British peremptorily rebuffed all requests for the diamond's restoration. Indian and Pakistani politicians may rave and pamphleteers may rant, but the British authorities remain adamant. The Koh-i-Noor is now kept in a glittering row of crowns in the New Jewel House built within the Tower of London in the spring of 1994.

The Darya-yi-Noor

Closely associated with the Koh-i-Noor is another, though less famous diamond, called Darya-yi-Noor, the river of light. It is now kept and exhibited in the jewel museum of the Central Bank (Bank-i Markazi) of Iran. It was brought to Persia in 1739 as part of the booty from Nadir Shah's Indian campaign, along with the Koh-i-Noor. During the unstable period following the assassination of Nadir Shah in 1747, it was held in turn by his blind grandson Shahrukh, Alam Khan Arab Kuzayma and Muhammad Hasan Khan Qajar and finally came into the possession of Karim Khan, the Zand ruler of Persia who reigned between 1750 and 1979.

In 1794 the Darya-yi-Noor was removed from the armband of Lutf Ali Khan, the last Zand ruler (reigned 1789-94) by Aga Muhammad Khan Qajar in Kirman; it was then inserted into the armband worn by successive Qajar kings. It was the favourite gem of Nasiruddin Shah, (1848-94). When wearing armbands became outmoded in the later part of his reign, he wore it variously on his watchband, chest, and hat. It was finally incorporated into one of the royal aigrettes (*jigha*), placed within a golden frame decorated with images of the Kayani (an ancient Persian dynasty) crown, two lions and suns ornamented with 475 small brilliants and four rubies. The next Qajar ruler, Muzaffaruddin Shah (1896-1907) wore it on his karakul cap during his European tour in 1902. When his successor Muhammad Ali Shah was forced to abdicate and took refuge in the Russian legation in Tehran, he took the crown jewels, including the Darya-yi-Noor, with him. He returned it to the Gulistan Palace Museum only under pressure from the Constitutionalists. The last two Iranian monarchs of the twentieth century Reza Shah, (1925-41) and his son Muhammad-Riza Shah, (1941-78), wore it on their military caps en route to their coronations.

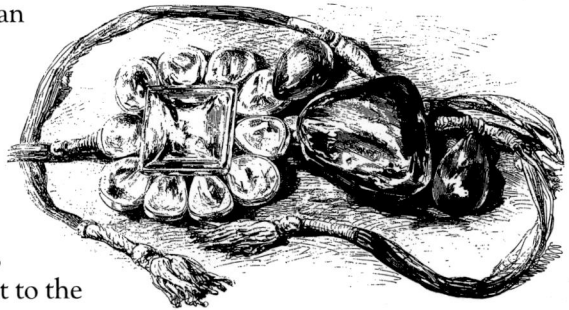

The Darya-yi-Noor as it was in Shah Jahan's collection

The Darya-yi-Noor is a flawless pink diamond, the sixth-largest-known in the world. It is a rectangular, step-cut tablet, 41.4 x 29.5 x 12.15 mm. Reports of its weight vary between 182 and 186 carats. One of the facets is incised with the words "al-sultan sahib qiran Fath Ali Shah Qajar 1250." At present the diamond is set in a frame 2.8 x 2.1.

In 1968, a team of Canadian diamond researchers led by V.B. Meen of the Royal Ontario Museum in Toronto concluded that "the Darya-yi-Noor is the major portion of the Great Table diamond seen by Tavernier in 1665." In May 1992, the Islamic government of Iran displayed with open pride the Persian crown jewels including the Darya-yi-Noor despite scorn from some of the puritanical segments of the Ulama.

Emerald Tiara of Golconda
origin. "The Crown Jewels of
Iran." Photography courtesy:
the Royal Ontario Museum

Opposite Page
The Darya-yi-Noor. National
Jewellery Museum, Tehran,
Iran. "The Crown Jewels of
Iran" Photography courtesy:
the Royal Ontario Museum

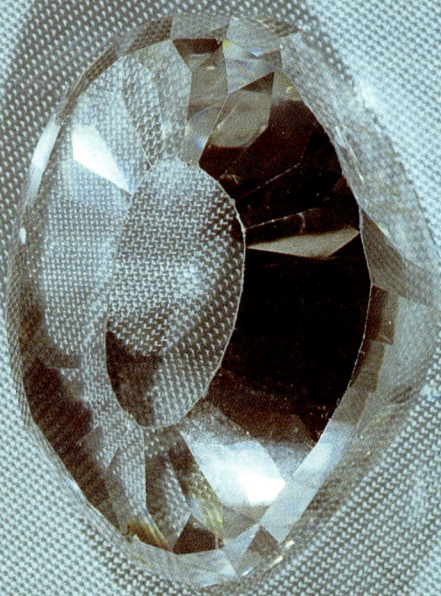

The Shah Diamond, with the Persian inscription "Burhan Nizam Shah, 1000 Hijri," corresponding to ca. 1591, of Ahmadnagar. Photograph. State Armoury Museum, Kremlin, Moscow

Opposite Page
Golconda diamonds in the National Jewellery Museum, Tehran, Iran. Taj-i- Mah, a colourless diamond of the finest quality can be seen on the lower left. "The Crown Jewels of Iran" Photography courtesy: Royal Ontario Museum

The Taj-i-Man and the Noor-al-Ayn

Two other Golconda diamonds are in the Iranian collection. The first is the Taj-i Mah '(moon crown),' an irregular Mogul cut of 115 carats. The second is the Noor-al-Ayn, Light of the Eye, which formed part of the tiara made by the New York jeweller Harry Winston of New York for Empress Farah Diba, the wife of the last Pahlavi Shah of Iran, Muhammad-Riza. The tiara made in 1958 consisted of an undulating band of colourless diamond baguettes, above which irregularly placed yellow, pink, and colourless brilliants held the Noor-al-Ayn in the centre. This superb and very limpid 10-carat stone is the world's largest recorded rose-pink diamond of brilliant cut and may have once formed part of the "Great Table." Yet another Golconda diamond that once formed part of the Persian jewel collection is the Shah diamond. The Shah is an interesting bar-shaped yellowish diamond weighing 88.7 carats, with three inscriptions that tell much of its history. It is a rare example of a stone carrying its own documentation. The first reads "Burhan Nizam Shah II in the year 1000." That Hijri year corresponds to common era 1591; the name is that of the ruler of Ahmadnagar in the Western Deccan, and an ally of the Golconda's Qutb Shahi sultanate. It may have been a gift from the Qutb Shahi ruler to Burhan Nizam Shah, as there is no record of diamond mines in the Ahmadnagar kingdom. The second inscription reads "Son of Jahangir, Shah Jahan, 1051," indicating that the stone was in the possession of the Mogul Emperor in 1641. Tavernier saw it in 1665 when he visited Aurangzeb. The third inscription reads "Qajar Fath Ali Shah." He was the king of Persia in 1824, so the diamond undoubtedly formed part of the jewels seized by Nadir Shah at the sack of Delhi and carried off to Persia. What did Burhan Nizam Shah use to make his diamond inscription, a difficult art? Obviously, a diamond as nothing else will work on a diamond, evidently diamond knives or diamond-pointed tools.

In 1829, Alexander Griboyedoff, the Russian ambassador in Tehran was assassinated. As "atonement" and as a "token of grief", the diamond was presented to Czar Nicholas I and became part of the Russian crown jewels. The diamond was rediscovered in 1922, and forms part of Russia's treasury of diamonds in the Kremlin, Moscow.

The Hope Diamond or Rama's Revenge

The Hope Diamond is one of the major precious stones available on public display in the Smithsonian Museum in Washington, D.C. It is renowned for its violet-blue colour and its fascinating history of bringing bad luck to its private owners. There is no doubt that it was one of the diamonds Tavernier brought back from India but just how he got it is something of a mystery. An English cutter charges he stole it from the eyes of a god named Rama-Sita and the bad luck that followed it is part of Rama-Sita's revenge. This same cutter, however, states that Tavernier himself suffered

Hope Diamond. Photograph: Natural History Museum, Smithsonian Institution, Washington, DC

from his theft; that he was devoured by wolves on the steppes of Russia. It is quite true that Tavernier died during a trip to Russia and may have been chased by wolves (although wolves are not in truth the man-hungry beasts legend has them) but it is also true that it was winter and Tavernier was 84 at the time of his death and could have died of a bad cold.

In any event, Tavernier first showed a magnificent blue, among other diamonds to Louis XIV in 1668 after returning from his sixth trip to India. Le Roi Soleil or the Sun King, as he liked to be known, Louis XIV liked practically all of the diamonds and he bought 45 large ones and 1,122 smaller ones, paying what amounted to about a third of a million dollars for the lot, and granting Tavernier a baronetcy in the bargain.

The blue was the largest. It was 112.50 carats and Louis XIV admired it so much he designated it "The Blue Diamond of the Crown." According to one of his mistresses, the Marquise de Montespan, he kept his prize jewels in a special closet of rosewood divided within "like cabinets of coins into several layers," and he was ever greedy for more diamonds, paying any price to get them. The Marquise shared his passions but feared the Blue as a harbinger of bad luck. It was first cut in Indian style but about five years after Louis XIV bought it he had the royal goldsmith cut it in the form of a heart. In 1774 Louis XVI inherited it and Marie Antoinette wore it, only to be guillotined in the revolution. When the French Revolution broke out, the tribunal placed the Blue, with other crown jewels, in a glass case in the Garde Meuble, listed it on the inventory and guarded it so carelessly that robbers—if indeed the robbers and the guards were not the same people— had little trouble carrying it off.

Unlike some of the other jewels, however, the Blue, also called the Blue Heart, was never seen again. It was probably sold in Spain and cut there into three smaller stones. The Goya portrait of Queen Maria Louisa shows her wearing a deep blue diamond cut much like the one that was offered for sale in London in 1830—now 44.5 carats of rounded oval. Henry Philip Hope, a rich banker, bought the diamond for $90,000; it was exhibited in the Crystal Palace, London in an exhibit that also showed up the Koh-i-Noor. Soon after it was recognised by Queen Victoria's jeweller Edwin Streeter as a piece of the Blue, but it stayed in the Hope family until the turn of the century and the legend of its sinister influence began again.

It was recalled that de Montespan had lost her place in court soon after wearing it, that Louis XIV had died a miserable death from smallpox, and that Louis XVI and Marie Antoinette had been executed. The Hopes themselves added to the stories: the original Henry Hope died without marrying, the nephew he left the stone to willed it to a grandson who changed his name to get it, but whose wife ran off with another man. The last of the Hopes went bankrupt and the stone was sold to a jeweller.

It changed hands frequently again in. A Folies' star who wore it was killed by her lover; a Greek broker who bought it fell off a cliff with his wife and children; the Ottoman sultan was forced to sell it when faced with revolution. And then Pierre Cartier the French jeweller bought it.

It was at Cartier's that Mr and Mrs Edward B. Maclean found it. He was the son of the millionaire publisher John R. Maclean; she was Evelyn Walsh, the daughter of a miner who, in her words, "struck it rich," and they each had $100,000 from their respective fathers for "something nice in a wedding present." Two hundred thousand was exactly the price Cartier wanted for the Hope, but Mr Maclean didn't want it enough to give up any part of his cash for it. Mrs. Maclean settled for another diamond but she still hoped for the Hope and when, a year later, Cartier arrived in Washington, D.C. with it reset in a necklace she raised $154,000 to buy it from him.

She loved it. There was no doubt of that.

Engraving by James Grant, 1822-87. Source: Cassell's *Illustrated History of India*, London: Cassell, 1876

A trail of misfortunes accompanied the arrival of the diamond. Their son was killed in an automobile accident, their daughter died of an overdose of sleeping pills, and Mr. Maclean himself suffered a nervous breakdown and died in a mental hospital; but while gossip said the Hope was their undoing Mrs. Maclean placed no stock in the legends about her diamond. She wore it almost constantly, stuffed it in a cushion when she didn't, and hired a detective to stand by on all occasions so that she wouldn't be robbed of it. At one point she pawned it to raise money to help find the Lindbergh baby, but the man she aided was the imposter Gaston Means. Many were the friends who handled her necklace; countless World War II American servicemen hospitalized at Walter Reed Hospital in Washington, D.C., whom she entertained with "look at it".

Mrs. Maclean died in 1947, a legend in her own time, and the Hope Diamond was bought by Harry Winston, with other jewels in her estate for more than $1,000,000. He first displayed it in his Fifth Avenue salon, then sent it on display about the country in charity shows, and in November

1958 mailed it to the Smithsonian Institution. The stamps cost him $145 — $2.44 for postage and the rest for insurance of $1,000,000. The United States Postal Service proudly put this event in a major advertising campaign in 1995. The diamond now hangs in a case in the American capital's famous museum. Rarely is the spot in front of the case empty and most who look at it, young and old, gasp before its splendour.

The Pitt-Regent Diamond

The Regent, the finest diamond in the French crown, is also called the Pitt diamond after its earliest known owner. The Regent's tale also begins in skulduggery. Its story begins with a sharp-eyed slave working in the Partiyala mines in 1701. In the rough, the diamond was enormous—410 carats—and when the slave spotted it he was willing to risk his life smuggling it out rather than simply turning it over to the Nizam's agent for a prize. Cutting a hole in his leg, he stuffed the stone into the wound, secured it by bandages and took off for Madras where he found a British skipper he thought he could trust. His mistake was fatal. The captain

The Pitt-Regent Diamond. Considered by some to be the most brilliant of all large diamonds. Musèe de Louvre, Paris

offered him an escape to freedom for half the value of the stone but once at sea, stole the stone and flung the slave overboard. Returning to shore, the captain then looked up a man named Jaychand, the largest diamond merchant in Madras at that time, sold the stone to him for £ 1000, squandered the money, and eventually hanged himself.

Jaychand now had a hard time selling the stone, partly because of its size, partly because it was stolen property rightfully belonging to the Nizam of Hyderabad, the East India Company's "Faithful Ally." It is possible that Thomas Pitt, who eventually bought it, knew this, for he drew a hard bargain with the merchant, a veritable diamond cut diamond situation! Pitt was the Governor of Madras, which had become a secondary market for Golconda diamonds, the primary being the peripatetic Mogul court. Having heard about "large diamonds to be sold," as he put it in a report, he invited Jaychand to come down to Madras as his guest. Jaychand brought the huge rough diamond with him but while Pitt bought some small ones, he balked at the £85,000 price which Jaychand asked for the big one. Over a period of months Jaychand came to and fro, trying to make a deal. He finally came down to £20,000 and the diamond was Pitt's. News of the stone got around slowly but get around it did and by the time Thomas Pitt returned to England some eight years later, he was being referred to as "Diamond" Pitt. Few believed he had come by it honestly, however, and repeatedly he had to answer slanderous attacks with an account of his purchase. Among others, Alexander Pope (1688-1744), the famous poet was supposed to point at something of the kind in the oft-quoted lines from the Man of Ross

"Asleep and naked as an Indian lay,
An honest factor stole a gem away;
He pledged it to the Knight, the Knight had wit,
So kept the diamond, and the rogue was bit."

It was hinted that Pope had originally written another last line:
"So robbed the robber and was rich as Pitt!"

Pitt sent the stone to cutters and it took them two years working by hand to cut it to the brilliant of 140.5 carats it is today. It cost him £25,000 to get the job done but he retrieved the dust, sold the stone for £70,000 and had the extra bits turned into some cuts Peter the Great of Russia bought. All together Pitt made a profit out of cutting but the job of selling the big diamond itself was difficult.

This was particularly so since Pitt suffered from a morbid fear of theft and murder. While carrying the diamond he disguised himself, never slept in the same house more than two nights, and if recognised; refused to show the diamond or admit he carried it. Finally, he sold it for £135,000 to the Duke of Orleans, then the Regent of France because Louis XV was too young to rule. The negotiations cost him £5,000, but he turned a tidy profit on the deal and with this he restored the fortunes of the ancient House of Pitt, a family which was soon to produce William Pitt who favoured fair treatment for the American colonies and for whom Pittsburgh, Pennsylvania, was named. Thomas Pitt himself, however, was not able to clear his name; seventeen years after his death his account of the original transaction was published for the second time by his son, to whom he had left the account in his will.

After its sale in France, the Pitt was called the Regent but its adventures were far from finished. In the royal inventory of the French court it ranked as the crown's most valuable stone—appraised at £480,000.

In 1792 when Louis XVI and Marie Antoinette were imprisoned, it was, like the other jewels, placed in the Garde Meuble and, like the others, stolen by the robbers who scaled the colonnades and shattered the glass case. Unlike the Hope, however, the Regent was immediately recovered from a ditch near the Champs Elysees in Paris. It was then sent to the Ministry of Finance who put it in a cellar but used it as a collateral on loans. When Napoleon came to power it was free of debt, and he had it set in the hilt of the sword he carried when crowned emperor. It stayed there until he went into exile to Elba, when Marie Louise, his wife, pried it out and took it home to Austria with her. Her father, however, made her send it back to Paris and Charles X of France wore it on his crown. When Napoleon III came to power he loaned it to Empress Eugénie. French queens are not crowned and cannot wear royal jewels, but she had it set for her hair in a Greek diadem, and dutifully left it behind her when she escaped from Paris in the carriage of her American dentist Dr Evans of Philadelphia. When the crown jewels were put up for auction in 1887 the diadem was kept back and placed in a case in the Louvre where it has remained in its Apollo Gallery —except for that period during World War II when the Germans occupied Paris; then it went into hiding in a stone-covered safety box at Chambord.

The Orlov or Orloff Diamond

Somewhat similar is the story of the Orlov (also spelled Orloff) diamond at least in the beginning. During the Karnataka wars in eighteenth century Deccan, a French soldier who had deserted Dupleix's army came to Srirangam, the site of an ancient and most important Vaishnavite temple city. The soldier learnt that the temple housed a statue of the god Sriranga, whose eyes were made of diamonds. One "eye" was especially remarkable. Of very pure water and with a slightly blue-green stone that gained it the name "Sun of the Sea," it was cut in the Indian rose fashion. Its form and dimensions were almost half those of a hen's egg, and it weighed 194.75 carats.

An ingenious plan soon took shape in the fertile and unscrupulous mind of the French soldier. After a number of patient attempts, he finally succeeded in convincing the gullible Brahmin priests to accept him as an adept in the temple's service. Alone one evening in the sanctuary, he easily removed the stone and at once set out for Madras, the nearest seaport, where he sold it for £2,000 to an English sea captain. The captain returned to England where he sold it for £12,000. It wound up in the hands of

Right
Black Orlov/Orloff diamond.
De Beers, London

Below
The Orlov/Orloff diamond
mounted on the imperial
sceptre of Russia. Photograph.
State Armoury Museum,
Kremlin, Moscow

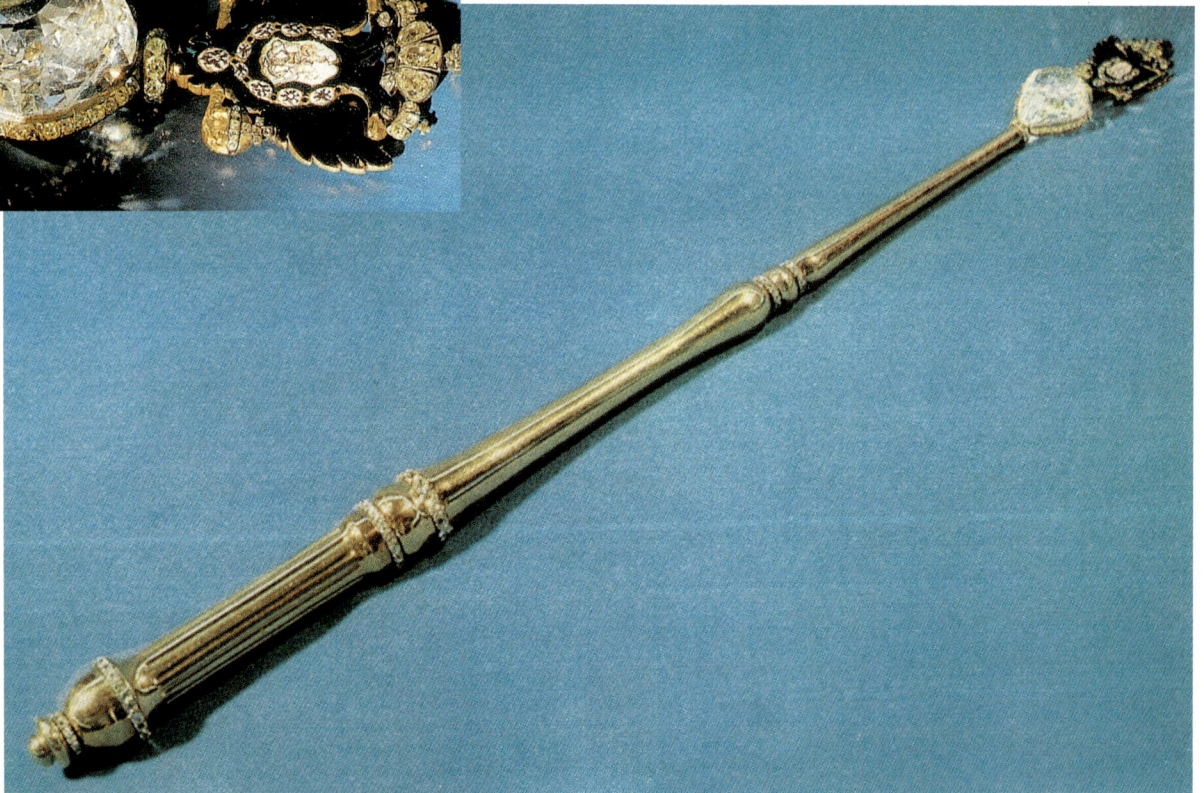

a Persian jeweller who in turn took it to Amsterdam, and in 1774 met Prince Orloff there and persuaded him to buy it as a gift for his Queen, Catherine the Great of Russia. That is how the diamond was named.

Prince Orloff was delighted with the chance. He was in Amsterdam because he had displeased Catherine with his handling of an Ottoman-Russian crisis—or perhaps she was just bored with him. They were not exactly a charming couple; she had been a German princess and she married Peter of Russia—whom most historians considered a foolish sort of fellow—solely to get the Russian throne. She got it too, declaring herself Empress the first time Peter went out of town, and then kept it with the help not only of Orloff but also his three brothers, all of them reputedly her lovers. At the feast of St. Catherine's Day in 1776, Gregory presented her with the jewel instead of the traditional bouquet of flowers. Graciously she accepted it but unluckily for the by now out of power and impoverished Orloffs, she did not reinstate Prince Gregory or his family in her favour.

As a final touch of irony, she had the diamond mounted on top of the double eagle in her imperial sceptre — the sceptre she would have neither won nor held without the Prince's early devotion, and his diplomatic skills. She preferred collecting jewels to men, however, and established her own cutting mills near the gem mines in the Ural mountains. She was said to wear 2,536 diamonds in her crown alone. When Orloff saw that another man had definitely usurped his place in the affections of the Empress, he became increasingly despondent and finally went mad. He was committed to an asylum, where he died in 1783. The diamond can be admired among the treasures in the Kremlin. There is another diamond bearing the name Orloff/Orlov. It is the Black Orlov/Orloff. It is described as 'dark gun-metal', which makes its Golconda origin somewhat suspicious as black diamonds are rarely found in Indian mines. Regardless of its origins, it is a remarkable diamond weighing 67.5 carats and cushion-shaped. Charles F. Winson (not to be confused with Harry Winston), a New York dealer, owned it for many years, exhibiting it at many events, including the display mounted by the American Museum of Natural History in 1951, the Texas State Fair in Dallas, and the Diamond Pavilion in Johannesburg in 1967. Winson sold the Black Orloff/Orlov in July 1969, then valued at a staggering $300,000 and set in a diamond and platinum necklace. It was sold again in December 1991 by Sotheby's in New York and is now believed to be privately owned.

The Idol's Eye Diamond

A story strikingly similar to that of the Regent is told of another Golconda precious stone called the Idol's Eye Diamond. According to *The GIA*

The Idol's Eye. Its colour is described as "a dazzling light blue tint."Musèe de Louvre, Paris

Diamond Dictionary, it was "among the striking and costly jewels of the late Mrs. May Bonfils Stanton of Denver, Colorado." It was a 70. 20 carat diamond of fine purity and colour. Its history starts in the early part of the seventeenth century when it was found in the famed Golconda mines. In 1607, the East India Company seized it from its owner, Persian Prince Rehab, in payment for his debts. It disappeared for 300 years and was rediscovered as the eye of a sacred temple idol. In 1906 it was reported to be in the possession of the Ottoman sultan Abdul Hamid. After several decades of ownership by different people, Harry Winston bought it in 1947 and sold it to Mrs. Bonfils Stanton, daughter of the Denver Post publisher. After her death it went in 1962 to Harry Levinson, a Chicago jeweller, who insured it for a million dollars with Lloyds of London, where Laurence Graff bought it in 1979 for his collection, but sold it after three years. The name Idol's Eye clearly suggests an analogy with the circumstances of the Regent diamond. Indeed, more than one American film is based on the theft of a diamond from the eyes of a Hindu god. For instance, in The Quest of the Sacred Jewel, a 1914 film, David Harding becomes fascinated with a priceless diamond set in the forehead of a stone god. He steals the diamond and escapes to America, but is followed by

Hindu priests who have observed his theft. In New York, Harding is killed by the priests, but they do not find the diamond. Harding leaves his fortune to May Rowland, his niece, who soon gives a party to celebrate her engagement to Joe Marsden. During the party, Joe is hypnotised by a Hindu priest disguised as an entertainer and after the guests leave, Joe is instructed to steal the jewel. May sees Joe take the jewel and calls off her engagement, but the case is eventually solved by a famous detective and his antic-prone office boy. The Hindus return with the diamond to the temple and May and Joe are happily reunited!

A more or less a similar plot was followed in another American movie of about the same time called A Prince of India, involving a famous diamond which brings ill-luck to all but the rightful owner. The Hope Diamond Mystery , a 1921 fifteen part serial film has nearly the same theme. Beginning in sixteenth century Golconda, it shows the tragedies the Hope diamond brings to those who are involved with it until it is returned to its rightful place in the breast of a Hindu idol. It appears that all three films are based on the nineteenth century English detective story *The Moonstone* by Wilkie Collins which itself was turned into a film in 1915.

Golconda-Graff diamond.
Graff Ltd., London

The Golconda and the Golconda d'Or Diamonds

A number of diamonds found in Golconda are found neither in Hyderabad nor anywhere else in the world. They are however recorded in reliable lapidary literature. According to *The GIA Diamond Dictionary*, cited earlier, two diamonds are named after the famous Golconda mines. One is the Golconda Diamond, described as a 30-carat emerald-cut diamond which was for many years in the "Collection of Registered Historic Diamonds" of Trabert & Hoeffer, Inc., New York City jewellers. Their description calls it "one of the last large diamonds from the old Indian mines." It was purchased by R. J. Reynolds, tobacco millionaire, in 1960, for $70,000 and given to Muriel Greenough who became the third Mrs. Reynolds. A fax sent to a firm of a similar name located in Chicago in May 1995 enquiring about the present whereabouts of the Golconda diamond received no answer. In a telephone conversation, the present owner of the firm Donald Levinson denied any knowledge of the Golconda diamond. The story of the other diamond, named the Golconda d'Or, follows a similar pattern. The Golconda d'Or was considered to be the largest emerald-cut diamond in the world. This historical stone was cut by Asscher of Amsterdam from its original 130 carats and weighed 95.40 carats afterwards. The Golconda d'Or is notable as one of the last large diamonds taken from the Golconda mines. It reportedly was handed down to the Ottoman sultan in the early nineteenth century. Evidently the Turkish dictator Mustafa Kamal sold the stone to a wealthy family. It was auctioned in 1962 by Sotheby's in London and purchased by Dunklings Private Ltd., the jewellers based in Melbourne, Australia. During an exhibition in Sydney Lower Town Hall in October 1980, it was stolen by thieves and has not been heard of since. As with most historic diamonds outside the museums, the chances of seeing it are rare for most people. In February 1984, the Graff Diamonds Ltd. of London reported that they had acquired a diamond called the Golconda/Graff, which weighed 47.29 carats. This cushion antique, brilliant-cut stone was the largest D-flawless of that shape graded by the Gemological Institute of America. No further information could be obtained from the firm despite several attempts in 1996.

The Hastings Diamond

The large diamond named after Warren Hastings (1732-1818), the British Governor-General of India, (1773-85), was sent by Nizam Ali Khan, the ruler of Hyderabad, to King George III in 1785. The diamond was sent through the former Governor-General who, about that time, was anxious to secure a favour from the king, as evidenced by a copy of a letter of the Nizam to Hastings found in the Andhra Pradesh State Archives. Hastings at the time was on trial in London for certain irregularities when in power.

Although acquitted, he landed into trouble as the courier of the jewel to the king, the circumstance of which was misconstrued. The report was soon spread that in order to prevent an adverse sentence, Hastings had bribed the king with a valuable diamond and, as Queen Charlotte had the reputation of being very avaricious, it was added that her mediation had also been purchased by similar means. One of the persons involved in the trial, Horace Walpole, commented: "I have not yet looked at the charges against Hastings, which fill a thick octavo. My opinion is formed more summarily: innocence does not pave his way with diamonds, nor has he a quarry of them on his estate." Evidently the diamond had arrived on the day after a crucial vote — to the delight of the opposition press, who at last saw nature imitating art. The event gave rise to numerous scurrilous writings and caricatures, which were publicly hawked about the streets and exhibited in shop windows. In one of these advantage was taken of a notorious charlatan who professed that he could eat and digest stones like an ostrich, and whose performances were advertised on posters under the heading of "The Great Stone Eater." For the juggler the caricaturists substituted the king, who was represented as "The Greatest Stone Eater." He was depicted with a diamond in his mouth, and a heap of others ready for mastication. Amongst the numerous street ballads that appeared on the occasion was the following, reprinted with some slight but necessary modifications by Thomas Wright (1810-87), in his *Caricature History of the Georges**

I'll sing you a song of a diamond so fine,
That soon in the Crown of our Monarch will shine;
Of its size and its value the whole country rings,
By Hastings bestowed on the best of all kings.
    Derry down, & c.

From India this jewel was lately brought o'er,
Though sunk in the sea, it was found on the shore,
And just in the nick to St. James's it got,
Conveyed in a bag by the brave Major Scott.
    Derry down, & c.

Lord Sydney stepped forth when the tidings were known,
It's his office to carry such news to the throne,
Though quite out of breath to the closet he ran,
And stammered with joy, 'ere his tale he began.
    Derry down, & c.

Here's a jewel, my liege, there's none such in the land,
Major Scott with three bows, put it into my hand,
And he swore, when he gave it, the wise ones were bit,
For it never was shown to Dundas or to Pitt.
    Derry down, & c.

"But run, Jenky run!" adds the king in delight,
"Bring the queen and the princesses here for a sight;
They never would pardon the negligence shown,
If we kept from their knowledge so glorious a stone."
                    Derry down, & c.

"But guard the door, Jenky! No credit we'll win
If the prince, in a frolic, should chance to step in;
The boy to such secrets of State we'll ne'er call,
Let him wait till he gets our crown, jewels and all!"
                    Derry down, & c.

In the princesses run, and surprised, cry "O, la!
'Tis as big as the egg of a pigeon, papa"
"And a pigeon of plumage worth plucking is he,"
Replies our good monarch, "who sent it to me!"
                    Derry down, & c.

Madam Schwellenberg peep'd thro' the door at a chink,
And tipped on the diamond a sly German wink,
As much to say, "Can we ever be cruel
To him who has sent us so glorious a jewel?"
                    Derry down, & c.

Now God save the queen! while the people I teach
How the king may grow rich, while the Commons impeach,
Then let nabobs go plunder, and rob as they will,
And throw in their diamonds as grist to his mill.
                    Derry down, & c.

* Published by Chatto & Windus, London, 1867.

Lord Pigot. Engraving by
Seawen after Powell.
[Source/copyright not known]

Hastings may have made the most of the part played by him in the transaction. He was fully aware that his enemies were both numerous and powerful, and great efforts were needed to command sufficient influence to obtain a favourable verdict. One of the means which he freely employed to secure this object was a lavish distribution of his funds amongst influential members of society. Hence he was not particularly interested at the time in refuting the popular impression that the great diamond was his personal, rather than the Nizam's gift to royalty. A certain amount of interest could not fail to be felt in the fate of a man who could afford to solicit the favour of his sovereign by such princely means. Society then was not immaculate as it is'nt now; every man had his price and that, when all else failed, diamonds ever commanded success! If he did not possess an unlimited store of these treasures, the impression that there were more where this gift to the king came from, might well serve his purpose. A fine stone weighing 101 carats, the Hastings is no longer traceable among the crown jewels, and no one knows what became of it. Some diamond historians speculate that the round brilliant in the Westminster tiara may be the Hastings.

The Pigot Diamond

This Golconda gem derives its name from Lord George Pigot, Governor of Madras, who received it in 1763 as a gift from the Nawab of Arcot, a vassal of the Nizam. It was a "small" diamond variously reported at 45 to 85 carats but handsome, a nice tribute to have, but it brought neither him nor his family luck. Pigot, after some sort of skulduggery, died in prison; his family put the diamond up for lottery, the winner sold it for a fraction of its worth, probably needing a little cash more than he needed a lot of diamond! It then came into the hands of Rundell & Bridge, the London jewellers, who were smarter; they sold it for $150,000 to Ali Pasha, an Albanian noble of the Ottoman court in Constantinople. The Pasha was said to have kept the Pigot in a pouch tucked in his sash, but it was no aid to his fortune. The Ottoman sultan sent an emissary to bring him to Constantinople for excessive ambition. He fought back and was fatally wounded. He requested permission to die in his own throne room, in his own fashion, and upon being granted this last request, he ordered that his two most precious possessions be destroyed: his Belowd diamond, the Pigot, and his wife, Vasilikee. A captain crushed with mighty blows the diamond to powder before his eyes but while his wife awaited her destruction, Ali Pasha died. Thus a number of Golconda diamonds were spirited out of the Deccan through fair means and foul, and some even destroyed by nobles like Ali Pasha.

The Arcots

Another major gift that the Nawab of Arcot gave to the acquisitive Queen Charlotte was five brilliants, the largest of which weighed 38.6 carats. This was oval shaped and subsequently set in a necklace with the two smaller stones. The other two diamonds were pear-shaped and were set as earrings; one weighed 33.70 carats and the other 23.65 carats. These two became known as the Arcot diamonds. After the Queen's death in 1818 the Arcots were sold to Rundell & Bridge, as per the deceased owner's will. They in turn sold them to the first Marquess of Westminster. A Parisian jeweller mounted the Arcots in the Westminster tiara, in a bandeau form, together with the round brilliant, and no less than 1421 diamonds. In June 1959, the third Duke of Westminster sold the tiara to help meet the cost of heavy death duties. Harry Winston paid £110,000 for it at a Sotheby's auction. Subsequently Winston had the two Arcots recut to obtain greater clarity and brilliance, the larger to 31.01 carats and the smaller to 18.85 carats. Each was remounted as a ring and sold to American clients in 1959 and 1960 respectively.

The Agra Diamond

Many Golconda diamonds ended up in the Mogul courts of Delhi and Agra and were even called "Mogul diamonds." By a treaty of 1636 the sultans of Golconda were required by the Moguls to pay a huge tribute, a part of which was in the form of diamonds. This explains the profusion of diamonds in Mogul jewellry and at the Mogul court. The Agra diamond is one such, named after the city of the Taj Mahal. It is 28.15 carats, light pink, in a modified-cushion-shape It was purchased by the Duke of Brunswick in 1844. Originally 46 carats, it was recut to 32.24 and was later owned by London's Bond Street jeweller Edwin Streeter, After his retirement in 1904, it was sold to Christie, Manson & Woods. The Agra was graded in 1990 by the GIA's Gem Testing Laboratory as Fancy Pink and sold by Christie's to the CIBA corporation of Hong Kong.

The Ahmedabad Diamond

The pear-shaped Ahmedabad (probably named after the city in which it was cut) diamond once belonged to Emperor Aurangzeb. It weighs 78.86 carats and was bought in Geneva by Robert Mouawad Jewellers on the 15th of November, 1995, when it was auctioned by Christie's. Evidently, it had come into the possesion of a Begum of Awadh who may have sold it to some Englishman after her kingdom's annexation by the East India

The Condé Diamond. De Beers, London

Opposite Page
The Agra Diamond. De Beers, London

Company in 1856. At the auction, Christie's did not reveal the source from where it had acquired the diamond for auction.

Le Grand Condé

This diamond is sometimes simply called the Condé diamond. It was probably purchased by Tavernier in one of the Golconda mines. Tavernier sold it to French king Louis XIII. It was given by Louis XIII to Louis de Bourbon, Prince de Condé. In 1886, the diamond was bequeathed to the French government by one of the prince's descendents. It is now on permanent exhibit at the Museé de Condé at Chantilly, France.

The Dresden Green Diamond

The Dresden Green is a 40.70 carat pear-shaped green diamond. The largest known diamond of this colour, it was originally purchased by Frederick Augustus of Saxony, Germany, in 1741 presumably from a dealer specialising in Indian diamonds. It is mounted in a hat ornament with several smaller diamonds, and is on display in the Green Vaults at the

Above
The Hortensia Diamond. De Beers, London

Right
The Sancy Diamond. De Beers, London

Dresden Palace in Germany. A gemological examination of the Dresden Green was undertaken by two senior staff members of the Gem Testing Lab of the GIA in November 1988. They were impressed by the exceptional transparency of the Dresden Green, reminiscent of that observed in colourless Golconda diamonds.

The Hortensia Diamond

This diamond derives its name from Hortense de Beauharnais, Queen of Holland. Together with other historical diamonds such as the Pitt-Regent and the Sancy, it is now on display in the Apollo Gallery of the Louvre Museum in Paris. It weighs 20.53 carats and is pale pink. Louis XIV of France purchased it from an unkown dealer. Stolen from the French Royal Treasury in 1792, it was recovered and later worn by Napoleon I and still later by Hortense de Beauharnais. It was stolen in 1830 again but recovered soon afterwards.

The Sancy Diamond

The Sancy is a 55-carat, pear-shaped, double-rose cut diamond. It derives its name from Nicolas de Sancy, a French minister (1546-1627). It has a long, complicated and confusing history, and in the words of Edwin Streeter, is "the very sphinx of diamonds." After centuries of being owned by several people, it was purchased by the Banque de France and Musée de France for the awesome amount of a million dollars from the fourth Viscount Astor. It is on display in the Louvre Museum's Apollo Gallery.

The Dresden Green Diamond. De Beers, London

The Shah Jahan Table Cut

The famed builder of the Taj Mahal and owner of the Takht-i Tawus, the Peacock Throne, collected a large number of precious diamonds, most of which no doubt came from the tribute that the Qutb Shahi sultans of Golconda were required to pay. Jewelled peacocks were prominent above the canopy of the throne from which the chair derives its name. It was a canopied gold throne 1.8 metres high and four metres wide, and studded with diamonds, emeralds, rubies, and pearls. Apart from this splendid throne, Shah Jahan also owned a beautiful 56.71 carat, octagonal, table-cut diamond, believed to be light pink. Depicted in a portrait by Nadiruzzaman, it is probably one of the "Three Tables" described by Tavernier. In 1739. The Persian tyrant sacked Delhi and carted away camel loads of wealth to his native land. In the stolen Mogul treasure were a number of diamonds possibly including the Shah Jahan. Two years later it was offered by the

Persians to Empress Elizabeth of Russia. More than two centuries later, on 16th May 1985, Christie's put up for sale in Geneva what was described as 'a spectacular historic diamond.' The man presenting it for sale claimed it to have been in his family since 1890s, it remained unsold.

The Wittelsbach Diamond

This is a 35.50 carat blue diamond and may have been brought to Europe by Tavernier. It was given by King Philip IV of Spain to his 15-year-old daughter Margareta Teresa when she married Emperor Leopold I of Austria in 1664. In 1720 it was bequeathed to the Archduchess Maria Amalia, who married Crown Prince Charles Albert of Bavaria. Wittelsbach was the prince's family name and that is how the gem acquired its name. When the country became a republic in 1931, the Wittelsbach and other items from the Bavarian crown jewels were sold at an auction. It disappeared briefly, then resurfaced in Belgium in 1962, and was sold to a private collector in 1964.

The Kirti Noor

Probably named to sound similar to the famous Koh-i-Noor, the Kirti Noor is at present the last of the Golconda diamonds to surface and become known in the twentieth century. It is a beautiful stone of a pink hue and was cut and polished in the early 18th century. There appears to be a great similarity of colour, shape, and grain to the Condé diamond; however, the Kirti Noor weighs 15 carats whereas the Condé is barely over 9 carats. The Kirti Noor was in the possession of an Indian prince before its sale to a Western dealer. A favourite of the prince, it was set as a centrepiece in a diamond necklace.

The Jettings

According to David N. Khalili, "diamonds, rubies, emeralds and pearls were the gems most commonly used in Mughal jewellery. Large gems were carved and shaped and used as centerpieces. Smaller stones were invariably cut en cabochon, though some examples of rose- or table-cut jewels are known from later periods. They were set in the kundan method. The Hindi word *kundan* means 'pure gold', and the name refers to the 24-carat gold that was used for the setting. A setting was gouged out of the metal, and the stone placed into it. A foil of pure gold was then folded over several times to form a narrow strip. One end of the strip was anchored by being pushed down between the stone and the setting flange. The strip was then pressed completely around the stone, and any surplus cut off. It was then burnished down all around the stone. When compressed, pure gold is completely weldable, even in a cold state. Thus the strip formed a

The Kirti Noor Diamond. De Beers, London

Opposite Page
The Shah Jahan Table Cut Diamond. Christie's Images, New York

Left
Turra, gold head ornament,
19th century Hyderabad.
Spink & Son Ltd., London

Below Left
Female adorned with jewellery
belonging to the Deccan
School, after originals in the
Prince of Wales Museum,
Bombay

Below Right
Pendent set with spinels and
diamond engraved with the
name Shah Jahan, 17th
century. Private collection,
Jerusalem. Photo by the Israel
Museum

Opposite Page
Jewelled dagger and sheath,
perhaps by Puran and Kalyan,
ca. 1619. Watered steel blade
studded with diamonds.
The al-Sabah Collection, Dar
al-Athar al-Islamiya, Kuwait
National Museum

Top
An important antique emerald and diamond sarpech. Designed as five graduated Table-cut diamond open floral panels suspending nine large emerald bead drops, the openwork tapering scroll aigrette W/ emerald and it's reverse.
Artist: 18th Century

Right
An important antique diamond and enamel sarpech. Designed as five graduated Table-cut diamond open floral panels suspending nine large spinal drops, and it's reverse.
Artist: 18th Century

Following pages (78-79)
An impressive antique emerald
and diamond pendant
Necklace. Endant W/ central
Table-cut diamond and two-
row floral borders and large
emerald bead drop to the low-
shaped mount and it's reverse.
Necklace W/ 42
Artist: Late 18th Century

Above
Gold & diamond necklace.
Thilo von Watzdorf Collection

Top
Guluband, nuptial necklace
with diamonds

Right
Gold armlet set with diamonds

Begum's Fan jabot pin with
Golconda diamonds.
© Hennell, London

Right
Nizam's Raansom brooch in
the form of a turban ornament
with Golconda diamonds.
© Hennell, London

Above
Peacock jabot brooch with
Golconda diamonds.
© Hennell, London

Jamuna necklace with
Golconda diamonds.
© Hennell, London

Above
Lotus bud jabot brooch with Golconda diamonds. 20th century jewellery. Hennell of Bond Street Ltd., London

Top Right
Moon drops necklace with Golconda diamonds. Hennell of Bond Street Ltd., London

Top Left
Crescent moon necklace with Golconda diamonds. 20th century diamonds. Hennell of Bond Street Ltd., London

solid wedge that held the stone in place. Further compression was sometimes added by means of a milligraining tool that produced a series of tiny bead-like granules around the edge of the setting, thus strengthening it as well as enhancing its effect. The *kundan* method is used in closed settings; for this reason, stones were often foiled to increase their colour and brilliancy. Coloured foils were often placed under crystal to simulate the effect of the more precious rubies and emeralds."

The fall in fortunes of Indian royalty, skullduggery, plain theft, and legitimate trade all contributed to the disappearance of the Golconda diamonds. It is ironic that not a single Golconda diamond of any value remains in the Deccan, all gifted or spirited away by unscrupulous sellers and dealers. Occasionally a few of the diamonds can be seen in the traditional jewellery still owned by Indian and foreign owners. Some jewellers in the West have made innovative use of Golconda diamonds by setting them in 20th century jewellery through a skillful and modern reinterpretation of traditional jewellery techniques. Examples of these can be seen in the products of Hennel 2" L's of Bond Street Ltd.

The Nizams of Hyderabad

Although many of the diamonds were lost, depriving the people of the Deccan of their natural heritage, the Nizams of Hyderabad were able to accumulate a fabulous collection of jewels unmatched by any other potentate in India. The Golconda mines were located within the realm of the Qutb Shahi sultanate, which became part of the Mogul Empire in 1687. After the death of Emperor Aurangzeb in 1707, the Mogul empire declined. New powers emerged in different parts of the country. The Mogul rule in the Deccan was menaced by the Marathas in the western part of the province. Finally, Nizam al-Mulk Asaf Jah, (reigned 1720-48) a Mogul grandee, dissatisfied with the conditions in the Empire, declared his independence in Aurangabad in or around 1720. The Golconda and Bijapur territories naturally became part of the new kingdom, which came to be known as the Nizam's Dominion of Hyderabad. For much of the eighteenth century, the Nizams and their dominion led a precarious existence due to recurring wars involving the Marathas in the North West and Tipu Sultan in the South. A succession of treaties with the East India Company ensured Hyderabad's security but at the price of subordination to the foreign power. It also involved cession of large chunks of economically-important fertile territory and strategically crucial sea-outlets. Given the usurpation of economically rich territories it seemed probable that the English would also seize the diamond mines located in the Nizams' domain. However, the Anglo-Nizam treaty of 1766 explicitly excluded from cession the region in which the diamonds were found and it remained in Hyderabad's control. The Nizam continued to acquire a small but regular supply of diamonds from the fields as attested by the reports of Benjamin Heyne. It is also evident from gifts, like the Hastings diamond, given by Nizam Ali Khan, (reigned 1762-1803) to George III, the British monarch in 1786.

On Nizam Ali Khan's death in 1803, Hyderabad emerged as a power although weakened militarily. Politically it was bound by a number of treaties with the English beginning in 1759. Although, its borders were secure, internal peace was not yet achieved. Bands of unruly Rohillas, Arabs, and Sikhs terrorised the peaceful citizens and exacted extortionate rates of interest on moneylending. Two large British-officered troops —

The British Residency at Hyderabad

The Subsidiary Force and the Hyderabad Contingent— lived in several cantonments. The Nizam was forced to pay for these forces, a needless burden. As the contemporary adage had it, "Nizzy paid for all." A low workload attracted many British men to the Nizam's territories to shake the infamous pagoda tree, which meant to make a fortune rapidly. So widespread was this phenomenon that this expression made its way into standard dictionaries of English. Secunderabad, the largest cantonment became the favourite stamping ground for the British buccaneers. Little wonder that Hyderabad state finances were in complete disorder by the mid-eighteenth century.

The mines in the Krishna and Pennar valleys no longer produced large diamonds regularly, although the Nizam occasionally received pleasant surprises. One such surprise took place in the 1830s, when a large diamond was found not in the mines but in a village near Shamsabad, not far from the capital. According to Richard Burton, "it was accidentally found by a ... *sonar* (goldsmith)... It had been buried in an earthen pipkin which suggests that it may have been stolen and was being carried for sale... The finder placed it upon a stone and struck it with another upon the apex of the pyramid. This violence broke it into three pieces, of which the largest represents about half... The discovery came to the ears of the celebrated *diwan* Chandu Lal. He very properly took it from the *sonar* before it underwent further ill-treatment, and deposited amongst his master's crown jewels, the Nizam diamond. The stone is said to be of the finest water. An outline of the model gives a maximum length of one inch 10'25 lines, and one inch two lines for the greatest breadth, with comfortable thickness

throughout. The face is slightly convex, and the cleavage plane produced by the fracture is nearly flat, with a curious slope or groove beginning at the apex. The general appearance is an imperfect oval, with only one projection which will require the saw: it will easily cut into a splendid brilliant, larger and more valuable than the ... Koh-i-Noor. I can hardly wonder at this stone being ignored in England and in India, when little is known about it in Hyderabad. No one could tell me its weight in grains or carats. The highest authority in the land vaguely said 'about two ounces or 300 carats.'

The Gemological Institute of America based in Santa Monica, California in its publication Diamond Dictionary gave its weight as 277 carats after cutting. It also claims that it may have been sold to an Indian banker for Rs. 70,000 although its value in 1857 was placed at £ 200,000. However, there is no indication of the diamond's present whereabouts. No independent verification of the claim is now possible in the absence of hard evidence. The Nizam Diamond was certainly not among the jewels sold to the Government of India in January 1995.

Hyderabad State incurred huge debts to the East India Company as a result of British skulduggery. In order to pay off the entire debt, Nizam Nasir al-Dawlah (1829-57) resolved in 1851 to pawn crown jewels up to the value of about half-a-million sterling. He contemplated forming a State Bank of Hyderabad to be financed by the leading moneylenders. It was to be managed by Henry Dighton (1799-1854), a British civil servant and merchant employed by the Nizam. Dighton spoke fluent Persian and Urdu, enjoyed the confidence of the Hyderabadis and the British alike, and was widely considered a sharp businessman. The choice of Dighton as the manager of the proposed bank was most appropriate as he was also in the good books of the Nizam's *Diwan* and the British Resident, the colonial diplomatic officer. To the bank, the Nizam agreed to hand over his jewels, and received in return an advance of 400,000 rupees. Contrary to all expectations, not only was the bank successfully founded, but the whole transaction was faithfully carried out: the jewels were handed over and the money was sent to the Nizam. Before, however, he had time to pay it over to the Resident, the British Governor-General in Calcutta interfered. He refused to sanction the formation of the bank on the ground that, as one of the directors was a European, it would be contrary to the Act of George III, which forbade all financial transactions between Europeans and Indian potentates. This order, which was unexpected, created a panic in Hyderabad. The Nizam, who had parted with his jewels, naturally held on to the money he had received, whilst the moneylenders who had handed over the money to the Nizam in the expectation of being able to recoup themselves from the State Bank saw no way of getting their investment back and wanted at all events to get the jewels as some sort of security. Dighton was thus placed in a very awkward position. He was responsible to

Opposite Page
The Grand Durbar in Delhi, 1903. The Nizam Mahbub Ali Pasha in the centre in a dark *sherwani* & white turban. When Lord Curzon asked him where his jewels were in this bejewelled assembly, he pointed to his nobles standing nearby

the Nizam on the one hand for the safety of the jewels, and on the other hand he was equally responsible to the moneylenders for the repayment of the money they had advanced. He managed to extricate himself from this dilemma in a remarkable and thoroughly oriental manner. The jewels were all kept in a safe in which were stowed different trays. The safe was locked with three different keys, each of which was kept by one of the persons interested. A meeting was called and a committee formed in order to establish an inventory of the jewels to see that all was correct. The safe was opened and each tray was brought before the committee, the jewels were counted and the tray was then carried back. But before they were replaced in the safe the contents of each tray were poured into a pair of jack-boots, the trays were placed empty in the safe, covered with their respective cloths and the safe was formally locked by the different members of the committee, while the jewels were carried up to Dighton's room. That same evening Dighton started in a palanquin of one of his attendants with a box marked medical supplies. In this way, carrying with him jewels to the value of half a million sterling, he managed to get out of the Nizam's Dominion. He soon reached Madras, got on board a ship, and safely took the jewels to the Netherlands, where they were deposited with a banking firm in Amsterdam, a major centre of the diamond trade. This firm advanced the money necessary to pay off the moneylenders. Upon his assumption of power in 1854, Salar Jang I, the great Diwan (1853-83), redeemed the jewels and had them brought back to Hyderabad and returned to the Nizam. In this novel way, no one eventually incurred any loss. The honourable conduct of Henry Dighton and Salar Jang I not only redounded to their renown but was a foundation of the credit which the Diwan enjoyed for the next 30 years. This was the first and only time in the Nizam's history that he had to pawn the crown jewels.

Writing in 1861, an early historian of the Nizams, H.G. Briggs, asserts that "almost all the finest jewels in India have been gradually collected at Hyderabad and are considered state property. The Nizam's private treasures are considerable. In jewels he is probably the richest individual in the world. One uncut diamond alone of 375 carats is valued at 30 lakhs (300,000) rupees, and has been mortgaged for half that money." He was probably referring to the recent pledge of the Nizam's jewels to obtain a loan from the local moneylenders. Briggs's statement may be considered the first disclosure of the Nizam's wealth and it constitutes the basis for the subsequent reputation of the Nizam as the richest man in the world.

Nizam Nasir al-Dawlah was succeeded by his son Afzal al-Dawlah, and he in turn by Mir Mahbub Ali Khan, popularly known as Mahbub Ali Pasha who reigned from 1869-1911.

The Diamond Paperweight

Mahbub Ali Pasha was by all accounts a popular ruler. He lived by turns in a number of great palaces in the city of Hyderabad, sometimes in the Chowmahalla palace, sometimes in the British colonial-style Falaknuma, and sometimes in Purani Haveli, the old palace. The stories of his charity are legendary as are the tales of his roaming in the town disguised as an ordinary man enquiring about the welfare of his subjects in a truly Haroon al-Rashid manner. He was perhaps the finest shot in India and once proved it to the doomed Archduke Ferdinand of Austria by repeatedly hitting a coin spinning in midair. His wide estates offered great sport, and in the heat of April or May when his jungles were dry, the Nizam would order his special train on a whim and rattle away to bag a tiger. The Nizam's longings could always be satisfied, since the train would keep up a head of steam and since all his palaces and shooting boxes were kept fully staffed. This was the best system, for it was his habit to announce a move without designating the location. He was generally dressed in an impeccable *sherwani* (long modern coat) and white pyjamas, though occasionally he wore European clothes; an English suit of elegant cut, glossy button boots, cravat, suede gloves, and frequently a gold-topped cane. But he was most at ease in the company of his boon companions with whom he indulged in parties. He enjoyed European spirits as well as the local toddy tapped from the abundant palm trees in his dominion. Indeed he sometimes acted as a toddy tapper or *kalal* on special occasions. But Mahbub Ali Pasha

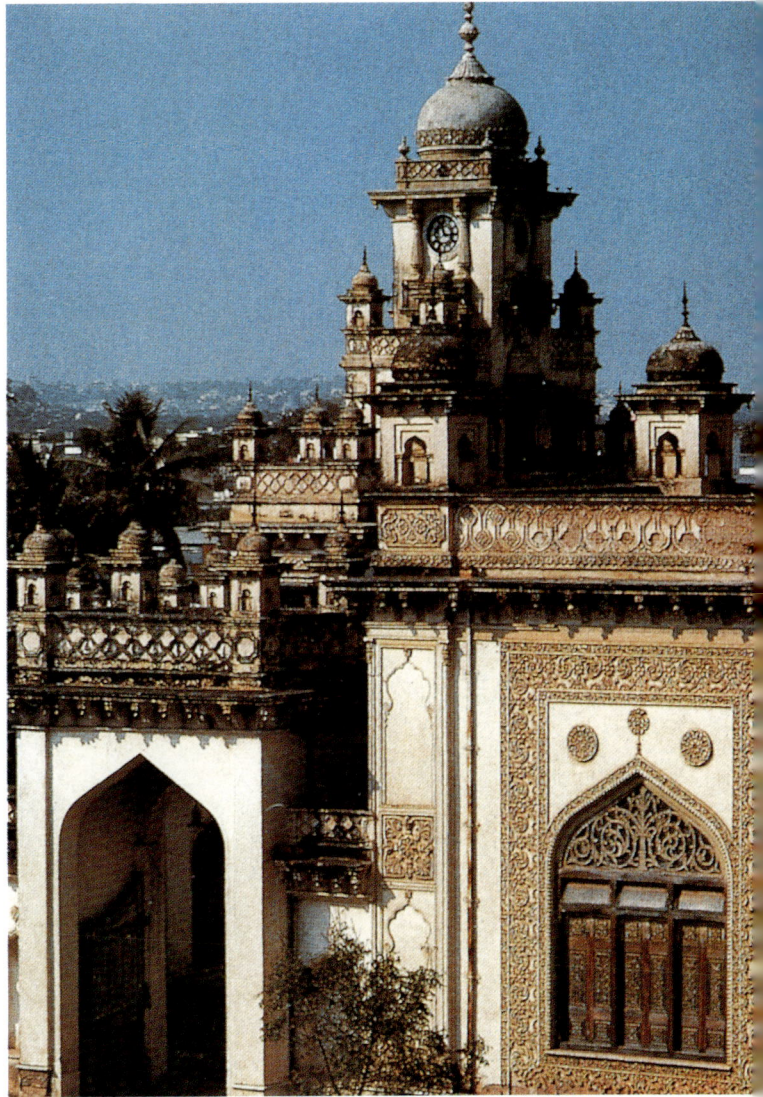

Chowmahalla Palace. Main gate and clock tower. Photograph by Omar Khalidi, 1996

could also surprise everyone with a deep interest in classical Persian and Urdu poetry. His tutor, *ustad* was no less than the towering poet Dagh Dehlawi, one of the last great masters steeped in the Mogul culture of the Red Fort.

In a matchless ode, the great poet Sarojini Naidu eulogized Mahbub Ali Pasha :

ODE TO H. H. THE NIZAM OF HYDERABAD
(Presented at the Ramazan Durbar)

Deign, Prince, my tribute to receive,
This lyric offering to your name,
Who round your jewelled sceptre bind,
The lilies of a poet's fame;
Beneath whose sway concordant dwell
The peoples whom your laws embrace,
In brotherhood of diverse creeds,
And harmony of diverse race:

The votaries of the Prophet's faith,
Of whom you are the crown and chief
And they, who bear on Vedic brows,
Their mystic symbols of belief;
And they, who worshipping the sun,
Fled o'er the old Iranian sea;
And they, who bow to Him who trod
The midnight waves of Galilee.

Sweet, sumptuous fables of Baghdad
The splendours of court recall,
The torches of a Thousand Nights
Blaze through a single festival;

And Saki-singers down the streets,
Pour for us, in a stream divine,
From goblets of your love-ghazals
The rapture of your Sufi wine.

Prince, where your radiant cities smile,
Grim hills their sombre vigils keep,
Your ancient forests hoard and hold
The legends of their centuried sleep;
Your birds of peach white-pinioned float
O'er ruined fort and storied plain,
Your faithful stewards sleepless guard
The harvests of your gold and grain.

God give you joy, God give you grace
To shield the truth and smite the wrong,
To honour Virtue, Valour, Worth,
To cherish faith and foster song.
So may the lustre of your days
Outshine the deeds Firdusi sung,
Your name within a nation's prayer,
Your music on a nation's tongue.

Like other princes of his time, Mahbub Ali Pasha was found of wine, women, and song. He lived a carefree and leisurely life, and spent a fair amount of time on *shikar*, big game hunting.

It was a summer afternoon, scorching hot. To Chowmahalla there came a Baghdadi Jew whose name was Alexander Malcolm Jacob. In that year, 1891, time had little meaning in the life of an Indian prince. The day was measured by the morning in which the sleepy palace gradually came to life, the afternoon in which it rested again, and the evening which drifted into the night.

A hansom drawn by a chestnut Arab horse brought Jacob to the palace gate. There the guards stopped him. Jacob alighted from the cab, wearing a white

Left
Falaknuma Palace Interior
view Collection: Omar Khalidi

Below
Chowmahalla Palace, exterior
view. Collection: Omar Khalidi

Far below
Chowmahalla Palace, iterior
view. Collection: Omar Khalidi

suit of superior shiny duck. Underneath it was a silk shirt. A pearl tie-pin rested uncomfortably on a coloured silk cravat, gaudy but expensive.

Jacob was on a special mission to the palace that day. He was sweating, partly because of the heat but also because of the excitement of meeting one of the richest men in the world. An appointment had been fixed for Jacob by the valet Aabid, after whom the famous road in downtown Hyderabad is named. Aabid held a privileged position in the royal household. By reason of his job he was closest to Mahbub Ali Pasha. He had the ear of His Highness and knew his royal master in all his off-the-record moods and moments. Aabid could be likened to a Gentleman-of-the Bedchamber. He was in fact the only one.

Aabid had easier access to His Highness than even the Diwan. The latter could only see the Nizam on business of state. Aabid was indispensable. Every time Mahbub Ali Pasha unfastened a button or changed a garment, Aabid was there. He had to be there. H.H. could not do without him.

Jacob, a soft, plump little black-haired man was characterised in three popular novels. Marion Crawford made him the protagonist of *Mr. Isaacs*; Crawford described Jacob over dinner at a New York club to his uncle Samuel Ward who encouraged him to write the story. Colonel Newnham Davis drew Jacob's picture in his less familiar *Jadoo*, and Kipling turned him into Lugran Saheb, the maker of spies in *Kim*. Jacob was notorious from Shimla to fashionable Paris for his powers and magic. The gullible credited him with the ability to walk on water and even the least credulous granted him powers of mesmerism and telepathy. It was generally believed by the Europeans and Indians alike that he practised white magic, and it was variously supposed that he was a Jew, an Armenian, a Russian agent, a British spy. It was obvious to all that he was the most important dealer in jewels and antiquaries in India, and known to a few that he had in fact undertaken missions for the Secret Department of the Government of India. He travelled by private train. His little store in Shimla was a pantechnicon of riches, blazing with gold and smoky with incense, and in it Jacob squatted, pale and subtle, keeping a diary full of secrets. It was Aabid who first spoke to the Nizam about Jacob and his precious stone. It had come by chance into Jacob's hands, who would not ordinarily part with it.

Mahbub Ali Pasha was naturally curious to see this diamond of which Aabid spoke. He would at least want to compare it with other priceless jewels in his own collection, part of which, by the most conservative standards, was rated as fabulous.

So the meeting was fixed for one afternoon the next week, and Jacob had come in response to that call. The guards knew of Jacob's arrival for, as was the custom, word had to be sent to the main gate before any visitor was allowed through it. His Highness would see him that afternoon, when he awakened from his mid-day siesta.

Jacob was escorted by a guard through the sprawling palace grounds. Past the squat buildings that had grown up haphazardly through the years he walked, mopping his brow. No one knew what his business was except Aabid who had brought him there. The curious eyes which peeped through slits of still curtains wondered who Jacob was. He was a newcomer to the palace. Perhaps he was a messenger from a foreign potentate, perhaps he was a banker negotiating a loan. But no one guessed the real purpose of his visit, which was to sell the largest diamond in the world to the only man who could buy it from him.

So he came to the inner courtyard of the palace where the Nizam lived. He mounted the seventeen steps that led to the long veranda and walked through the archway, which rested on long columns, to the main audience room. There he waited.

Below his feet was an old Persian rug, woven as finely as petit-point embroidery. Around him, as he cast his eyes about, he could see a mixed assortment of furniture which had come from all parts of the world. It looked Victorian. The hall was large.

The escort left Jacob there, awaiting His Highness's pleasure. From another room a palace servant pulled the cords of a primitive Indian ceiling fan called a *punkha* to keep Jacob cool. There he sat, in solitary splendour, emotionless. He showed no sign of nervousness even though an 182 1/2 carat diamond nestled in the inside pocket of his coat. Occasionally, his hand went, almost instinctively, to it; it was just his habit of making sure the gem was still there.

There was stillness about the great hall. The Nizam was asleep. Everyone walked on tip-toe, for His Highness's retiring room was just behind the heavy silk curtains.

Then Aabid came. He went up to Jacob and greeted him warmly, as merchants do on the eve of big business. They spoke for a while in

Falaknuma Palace. View of the smoking room. Photograph by Omar Khalidi, 1996

The Diamond Paperweight

low whispers, not out of habit but merely to fit in with the pattern of palace life at this hour. Intrigue, it is said, is in the air of Hyderabad, and petty jealousies haunted the *havelis* (palaces) of the Indian princes. This had made it incumbent on all who valued their life and safety of position to speak always in whispers so that no one else could hear. The habit had far outlived the necessity.

Then Aabid left, for there were signs of His Highness's, awakening in the room next door. Soon he would give an audience to Jacob. It was the only appointment His Highness had that afternoon. Affairs of state had all been settled earlier in the day.

Mahbub Ali Pasha was at peace with the world. His 'world' was really only the British Resident. The Resident represented the Viceroy of India, who in turn represented the British monarch. With the British, the Nizams had treaty rights. He had no doubt in his mind that these rights would be respected so long as the good Queen Victoria ruled in England. Her name

Jacob Diamond. Photograph by Prashant Panjiar, *India Today*, 1995

stood for progress, steady but sure, which moved from precedent to precedent with the cadence of a Tennysoni on Tennysonian stanza.

The wars with the British were over. The Uprising of the 1857 War of Independence lay half-a-century behind. The Nizam's dynasty had stood the British test of loyalty. It was he who first stood with the British against the rebelling hordes. It was he who paved the way for the restoration of law and order. The British would never doubt the House of Nizam.

Jacob was already standing up, even before the Nizam had entered the big hall. He bowed humbly and low. In that lowly position he remained till His Highness came up to a chair near him and sat down. Then Jacob raised his head.

Throughout the meeting Jacob remained standing. It was the ritual of the Court. Eagerly he waited for the drop of His Highness's words.

Nothing happened for a quite a while. Aabid adjusted the table near the Nizam's chair and helped his royal master with his rings, as he had always done. Fresh from his sleep, always immaculately dressed whether for a formal reception or an informal meeting with a jeweller, the Nizam looked at Jacob for the first time and nodded once or twice. He was merely summing up the man who had a jewel of which there was said to no other like it in the world. Then without further ado, His Highness asked to see it.

Jacob's hand went to his coat pocket. This time the outer one. From it he produced a red velvet cloth and spread it on the table which Aabid had placed nearby. Then he produced from the inside pocket a packet wrapped in a handkerchief of ordinary white cloth. Carefully he unfolded it, till he came to a parcel of red tissue paper such as Indian jewellers use to wrap their wares.

He put the handkerchief aside. Then he proceeded to unwrap the red paper packet. From it he produced the gem and placed it on the velvet cloth. There it lay like a duck's egg with a flat bottom. It was pure white and of an English cut, weighing 182 1/2 carats, found in the Kimberley mines of South Africa, in 1884 and initially called the Victoria Diamond.

The Nizam looked at it for a while. He picked it up and examined it in an off-hand way. His face registered little amazement but much pleasure. He placed it on a finger to see how it would look set in a ring. But he cancelled that image. It was too big for that, he seemed to say.

"Aabid!' he called to his valet nearby and Aabid moved forward in an instant. 'Put it on your shirt."

Aabid did as he was told. The Nizam looked at it for a while. Could it be worn as a button on the *sherwani* he wore on state occasions, he wondered. Then he shook his head. It would be difficult to match it with five more of the same kind, which such a coat would require.

Aabid placed it on the table again, but removed the red cloth which was below. Instead, he put under it a letter which was lying by. The idea appealed to the Nizam. The 182 1/2 carat diamond could be used as a paperweight, as his valet had ventured to suggest. He nodded to Aabid who knew what the nod meant.

Aabid smiled gently at Jacob who, unaccustomed to these long restraints, burst into a broad grin which ran across his face. Jacob mopped his brow for the last time. His troubles were over. The deal was complete. Aabid took Jacob's diamond into the inner room to which the Nizam retired while Jacob remained still bowing low to His Highness the Nizam. Aabid would attend to the details, for the Nizam's nod was his command. Back along the quadrangles Jacob walked to the main palace gate where his chestnut Arab was still waiting for him to return.

The "details" did not work out as smoothly as Jacob had expected. Soon after the deal that summer afternoon in the Nizam's palace a money dispute arose between Jacob and Aabid. The matter went to court. The British Resident, always looking for intervention, was made aware of it and, as the matter could not be settled without reference to His Highness, for he was concerned in the deal, his evidence, which had a vital bearing on the dispute, had to be heard.

The Nizam of Hyderabad, as a ruling prince, had sovereign powers. He could not be summoned to appear as a witness in any ordinary court. But the British Resident had to request His Highness 'to be pleased to appear' at the Residency to give his evidence to the commission. While couched in terms of a request, appearance was an obligation by protocol. The Resident spoke in the name of the Viceroy of India, who in turn represented the British Crown. The Nizam had no option but to accede to the Resident's humble request. It was indicated to the Resident that His Highness "would" be pleased to give evidence.

But to Mahbub Ali Pasha, it was an inauspicious omen that anyone in his exalted position should have to drive to the office of the Viceroy's deputy to appear in person to give evidence in an ordinary money dispute. In his own courts the Nizam was both judge and jury, the final dispenser of justice, the sole arbiter of what was right and what was wrong. His word was law and his subjects had been brought up to regard it as such. To be called, even requested, to appear in person at the Residency was an insult. It was a blow to his prestige from which he could not easily recover. Jacob's diamond had brought him bad luck.

The Nizam gave the required evidence in the case, but when he returned to the palace that day he went straight to his room to wash his hands. Then he went to his desk and picked up the paperweight to which he had now taken a dislike. He ripped off the nib-cleaning cloth, wrapped the 182 1/2 carat diamond in it, and slid it away into the writing-table drawer. There it remained for many years for nobody knew he had done this, until his successor Mir Osman Ali Khan (reigned 1911-48) discovered it by accident in the toe of his father's slippers in Chowmahalla Palace. Osman Ali Khan did not have the same superstition which his late father did. He had it mounted on a gold base of filigree work and put it away in a yellow box. The Aga Khan III is said to have offered nearly a £ 1000,000 for it. But it was not to be sold in Osman's own lifetime.

As for Jacob, although he won the case against the Nizam and saved his investment, he was broke. His legal expenses were great. No prince in India would deal with him again and he died in penury, even his magic spent, in Bombay.

The Richest Man in the World

"About the time that the Nizam's ancestor Khwaja Aabid Khan trekked to Delhi..." the English poet John Milton had sung

"The wealth of Ormus and of Ind
Or where the gorgeous East with riches hand
Showers on her Kings barbaric pearl and gold."

In the first half of the 20th century, the sole remembrance of that world of which the poet sang, and which so fired the imagination of the Western world that Columbus and other navigators sailed round the globe, was in the person of Osman Ali Khan, the last Nizam of Hyderabad. He was thought to be the richest man in the world. He probably was not. No one was ever able to fully count all the money he had in ready cash, gold bars, *ashrafis* (gold coins), diamonds, palaces, crown lands, and real estate. The estimates of his private wealth at his death in 1967 swung wildly from a hundred and sixty million pounds to six hundred million. According to D. F. Karaka, a Bombay journalist, the Nizam's personal wealth was estimated at approximately one hundred million pounds sterling. Of this, £ 25,500, 000 was in liquid cash, £ 35,000,000 in jewellery and a like amount in real estate. These figures were, Karaka cautioned, only approximate, for those who are close to the Nizam are not very communicative on the subject.

In addition to the personal wealth, the Nizams have always owned crown lands known as the Sarf-i khas. The estate itself was estimated to be worth about £ 70 million. The management of the Sarf-i khas has always been in the hands of the rulers. The estate devolved from generation to generation in direct descent from the first Nizam. It was an appendage to the throne. As in the case of a baronetcy or peerage trust, the purpose of the Sarf-i khas was to ensure that the incumbent would be able to maintain the dignity of the dynasty. The income from the Sarf-i khas belonged to the ruler for life. He could do as he liked with it, but he could not alienate any part of the property itself.

State property was distinct from this. It was referred to as *Diwani*, meaning that which was administered by the *Diwan*, or minister. Diwani property

Nizam Mir Osman Ali Khan

belonged to the government. From its revenue the state was administered; from it also the ruler received his privy purse which, in the case of the Nizams, was fixed at £ 350, 000 in the early 20th century.

In his own lifetime, the wealth of the Nizam Osman Ali Khan was equalled and surpassed by many in India and elsewhere. It was his liquid cash, which for many years lay in his coffers, and his jewels, that were difficult to match. The wealth of the well-known millionaires and billionaires is usually locked up. That of the Nizam was easily convertible into cash. That was his power, and weakness. For instance, according to *Newsweek* dated 12 September 1955, "rats ate their way through a reported $8.4 million in Indian bank notes stashed in rotted trunks in the palace

Main street in Hyderabad.
19th century drawing.
© Omar Khalidi

vaults." The government in New Delhi refused to issue new currency notes upon his request.

Apart from his liquid cash and jewellery, Nizam Osman Ali Khan was reported to have large quantities of gold. Osman Ali Khan's successor and grandson Prince Mukarram Jah (b. 1932), referring to a 1963 regulation that prohibited possession and sale of gold over a certain quality and quantity, told an American academic in 1971 that his grandfather's "response to the Government of India's Gold Control Order was to declare his holdings at about 22 tons." This statement fits in with the popular gossip that the Nizam left gold bars scattered like kindling wood around the palace yard. C.B. Taraporewala, (d. 1969), the Nizam's financial advisor once told a journalist that the Nizam had "about forty thousand rare gold coins—and I presented them to Prime Minister Lal Bahadur Shastri. I told him each coin is worth one hundred times its face value. Shastri said ' Very good', but not a word of thanks. The government never thanked the Nizam." Taraporewala also mentioned that the Nizam had gold plates for hundreds of guests.

Pearls made an important part of his collection. According to Justice V.K. Reddy, whose grandfather was the famous *kotwal*, or commissioner of police, Raja Bahadur Venkata Rama Reddy, one fine morning the Nizam said to his *kotwal*, 'Rama, I think it's high time we sorted out the pearls.

"So they went to the treasury and there they pulled out buckets and buckets and buckets of pearls of all shapes and sizes. They washed them in a solution of boric acid and used a sieving system for grading gravel to categorize their size. Finally he had the pearls sorted according to quality and laid them out to dry on huge sheets that were spread over the entire palace roof."

Lieutenant-General His Exalted Highness, Nawab Sir Mir Osman Ali Khan Bahadur, Regulator of the Realm, Victorious in Battle, Aristotle of the Age, Shadow of God, and Faithful Ally of the British, to give the barest hint of the Nizam's titles, was every inch a king. Five feet three inches tall, and slender to the point of delicacy, fine-boned and smooth-skinned, he retained the look of youth long past middle age through nearly four decades of rule. Immaculately dressed in an elegantly tailored *sherwani* topped by a ruby red fez, he was like a relic from the Mogul age. In the early years of his reign he was fond of riding and polo. His harem was large. Probably the only first-hand account of this harem recorded is by Brinda, the beautiful Spanish maharani of Kapurthala, a Punjab state. According to Brinda, on a visit to Hyderabad, "The Nizam led me along endless corridors which twisted and turned and wound about through the palace. We walked silently up and down the long flights of stairs, through curved archways and carved doorways... At last we came into a room almost the size of the ballroom at Buckingham Palace... There, before me, standing practically at attention, stood over two hundred women. All were lovely-looking with dark eyes, slim supple bodies, and golden skin which shone like satin. They were exquisitely dressed in sparkling brocades and shimmering silks, and gold bangles and jewelled bracelets on their arms and wrists. They were undoubtedly the most beautiful women I had ever seen." Earlier the Nizam had given Brinda and her husband a grand banquet and presented her "a magnificent necklace of diamonds, emeralds and pearls. I gasped when I saw it." Strangely, the Nizam became more frugal and religious as he grew older. He was revered and respected throughout India and the Muslim world as a pious ruler in the tradition of the Khulafa-i Rashidin, the four Rightly Guided Caliphs. The Nizam's personal religious regime was rigorous. He regularly went down to the Bagh-i Aam mosque in an old car and worshipped there among his people without seeking or being accorded any distinction. Every evening at six he prayed alone beside his mother's grave. By his frugal habits and his distaste for pomp and ceremony, Osman Ali Khan became

Charminar, the emblem of Hyderabad built in ca. 1591

the target of the yellow press all over India and England, where gossip columnists vied with each other for the most bizarre stories about him and his "filthy lucre."

Hyderabad, the capital of the state, was a truly cosmopolitan city. Its many gardens, lakes, fine palaces and mansions, clean wide boulevards and bridges made it a true metropolis. Scholarship, the pursuit of poetry, the collection of fine art and the practice of brilliant conversation were common among the noble families. In the memorable words of the Nightingale of India, Sarojini Naidu;

NIGHTFALL IN THE CITY OF HYDERABAD

See how the speckled sky burns like a pigeon's throat,
Jewelled with embers of opal and peridote.
See the white river that flashes and scintillates
Curved like a tusk from the mouth of the city-gates.

Hark, from the minaret, how the muezzin's call
Floats like a battle flag over the city wall.
From trellised balconies, languid and luminous
Faces gleam, veiled in a splendour voluminous.

Leisurely elephants wind through the winding lanes,
Swinging their silver bells hung from their silver chains.
Round the high Char Minar sounds of gay cavalcades,
Over the city bridge Night comes majestical,
Borne like a queen to a sumptuous festival.

The Jeweller Felt Dizzy

The many works of public benefit created during the last Nizam's reign testify to his interest in the welfare of his subjects. One of the finest British architects of the time, Vincent Esch, designed some of the best buildings that adorn the city. The High Court, Osmania Hospital, City College, Asafiya State Library, and Jagirdars' College (now the Public School) are some of his masterpieces.

Far away from the din and noise of the city, the Nizam commissioned Belgian architect Ernest Jaspar to design a magnificent building for Osmania University. Apart from public welfare, the Nizam had only one passion: the hoarding of money; cash, gold coins and bars, diamonds, and jewels. The Nizam augmented an already rich inheritance with purchases from fallen European royalty like the Russian czars. A wealthy jeweller described to D. F. Karaka, his experience of the Nizam's jewels when he visited him during the Second World War. Money was easy to come by at that time and the jewellers of India were doing a roaring trade with a new crop of the newly-rich rising out of the black markets of India buying expensive jewels alike for wives and mistreses. Even so, it was not too easy to find a buyer for the two beautiful 25-carat rubies which had come into the hands of the jeweller. Someone suggested to him that he should show them to the Nizam of Hyderabad.

With suitable introductions, the jeweller arrived in Hyderabad one day, carrying the rubies on his person. He stayed in the city as a guest of one of the Nawabs whose father and grandfather had been in close touch with the royal house, having loyally served two generations of Nizams.

Through his host an audience with the Nizam was sought. This was granted. A day or two later, suitably attired in his best London-cut suit wearing a silk shirt and moiré tie, heavily lavendered, the jeweller arrived with the two rubies at the palace. After the formal courtesies were exchanged between the jeweller and his prospective buyer, the Nizam asked to see the rubies which had been so highly praised to him.

Quickly the jeweller produced them from his inner pocket and proudly laid them before the Nizam. The Nizam looked at them closely, betraying no astonishment at their purity or size. Without saying another word he signalled to his attendant to come over and in a low voice gave him a command. The palace official whisked away to do his bidding.

Not much was said until from another part of the palace a large steel trunk arrived which was placed near the feet of the Nizam, who asked his attendant to unlock it. The trunk appeared to be full of little bags of no particular charm or attraction. They were virtually dumped together and the trunk was full of them.

After looking carefully for a few minutes at this assortment of bags, the Nizam picked one up and untied its cord. He dipped his hand into the bag and drew from it some two dozen rubies of various shapes and sizes which he put on the table for the jeweller to see.

"It was like a schoolboy producing marbles from his pocket," the jeweller said. 'I became quite speechless. In comparison with what he produced, the two beautiful gems which I had brought with me looked mere baubles.'

When the jeweller regained his voice he expressed his amazement and admiration at the rubies laid before him. The Nizam smiled and looked into the trunk again. He picked up another bag and from it he extracted a handful of emeralds. From yet another he drew pearls, and so on until almost every precious gem, each of incomparable beauty, lay before the astonished jeweller's eyes.

Nor was this the only trunk. For this fabulous wealth, inestimable by anyone, had been lying for years unset and unmounted, like pebbles, in bags stored in various trunks in the palace strongroom. No jeweller can ever value such priceless gems for if they were put on the market all at once, they would wreck it.

After a few minutes the Nizam modestly asked the jeweller for his opinion of some of the stones. The jeweller, mopping his brow, frankly admitted that he was feeling dizzy. The Nizam then politely said, "You see, I have no immediate need for rubies at present. Your stones are very good. You should get a very good price for them."

With the exchange of a few more formal courtesies, the audience with the Nizam was over. When the jeweller stepped into his car he noticed that his tie had slipped below his collar and his feeling of dizziness persisted. Yet this was one of the leading jewellers of India, accustomed to handling beautiful jewellery ever since he was a boy and who could count among his clients some of the richest princes in the country.

The Nizam served the British Crown most faithfully. He had been on the throne for three years when World War I began: he sent two regiments of lancers to guard the Suez Canal. The Nizam was richly rewarded with a title of His Exalted Highness, in contrast to the mere His Highness of other maharajas. A quarter of a century later his troops again went to war for the British in Europe. Not long after the end of World War II the faithless British deserted their faithful ally in the hour of his greatest need against the new government installed in New Delhi in mid-August 1947. For a year a fog of rumours and alarms drifted over Hyderabad. The Rizakars led by Qasim Rizawi wanted Hyderabad to become a Muslim state, the communists wanted to turn it into a Red Republic, while the Hindu extremists desired nothing short of a saffron Ram Rajya. The Nizam preferred to remain an independent sultan*.

A new relationship between the Nizam and the Government in New Delhi had to be established. This was done by a letter written by the military governor dated 1st February 1949. The proposals made in this and subsequent letters were later incorporated into a formal agreement on 1st January 1950 between the Indian Union and the new State of Hyderabad on the one hand, and the Nizam of Hyderabad on the other.

The agreement guaranteed to the Nizam all the personal privileges, dignities and titles enjoyed by him within or outside the territories of the state immediately before the day of Indian Independence, i.e. 15th August 1947.

He was guaranteed an annual privy purse of Rs. 5,000, 000 free of taxes. A further sum of Rs. 2,500, 000 was guaranteed to be paid to him every year for the upkeep of his palaces, and another Rs. 2,500, 000 annually in lieu of income hitherto received from the Sarf-i khas estates.

There was an additional annual payment of Rs. 2,500, 000 guaranteed by way of a civil list for the two princes, two princesses, two grandsons, and the brother of His Exalted Highness.

An annual payment of Rs. 12,500, 000 was solemnly guaranteed by the Military Governor who was acting under instructions of the Indian government.

Four years later, India's Prime Minister Jawaharlal Nehru wrote a personal letter to the Nizam which began with the ominous words "Dear Friend." The superstition is that each letter from Nehru which begian with the words 'Dear Friend' cost the Nizam a tidy fortune. Friendship with India's Prime Minister was a "most expensive business" the Nizam once remarked.

In his letter Nehru pointed out to His Exalted Highness, as he did to a hundred other maharajas of India, that the privy purse of the princes had become an "anachronism" in the context of India's economy. His "Dear Friends" should therefore accept a voluntary cut.

*After months of negotiation, the Government of India annexed Hyderabad in a military exercise called Operation Polo.

The Nizam replied —always with due respect — that he failed to see how a solemn agreement in 1949 could become an anachronism in 1954. To this, Nehru had no reply.

With regard to the Rs. 2,500,000 paid annually to the Nizam in lieu of his former income from the Sarf-i khas, C.B. Taraporewala, in his ponderous financial prose said:

"It would be interesting to ascertain to what extent this compensation was fair and reasonable. As it happens the private estates and properties comprised in the Sarf-i khas used, prior to their merger in the Diwani (in 1949), to yield a net surplus, after deducting the expenses of the administration... of nearly Rs. 12,400,000 per annum. The sum of Rs. 2,500,000 thus represents only a fifth of what was due to the Nizam. No compensation in cash or bonds worth the name was ever offered to the Nizam for the surrender of these rich and vast properties. Both the Constitution of India which provides for reasonable compensation, and the Jagir Abolition Regulation (JAR) of the Hyderabad State provide standards which could well have been applied. Under the provisions of the JAR the purchase price to be paid by way of compensation would have been the equivalent of ten years' income. With a yearly net income of Rs. 12,400,000, the compensation for the Sarf-i khas would therefore have amounted to Rs. 122,500,000. Even if that amount had not been paid all at once, but had been spread over twenty equal annual instalments, the annual compensation to the Nizam would have been something like Rs. 6,250,000 for twenty years and not Rs. 2,500,000 for his lifetime alone.

What is more amazing is that the State having taken over these assets and properties, did not, however, take over the obligations that had hitherto been charged upon them. Out of his income the Nizam had been maintaining not only his own family but a large number of other dependents, including the former dependents and servants of his predecessors. Such dependents now number over 14,000 and include many widows, Scheduled Caste women and other helpless persons."

Even though the Nizam has felt the loss of a crore of rupees from the Sarf-i khas, he has not relinquished his guardianship of these dependents. "They are human beings whom he cannot write-off," the financial advisor said.

He then revealed that the promised annual payment of Rs. 2,500,000 to the two princes, two princesses, the two grandsons and the Nizam's brother "had never been made."

In view of the uncertainty which faced his family, his heirs and dependents and such charitable causes as he wished to safeguard during and after his lifetime, the Nizam decided to liquidate part of his wealth and transform it into a series of trusts which would achieve this object.

He created 33 such trusts. Heading them are the trusts for his two sons, Azam Jah, Prince of Berar, and Prince Muazzam Jah, each for the sum of Rs. 18,200,000. The senior Prince died in 1970, and the junior in 1987. Other important trusts included the ones for jewellery and the two grandsons Prince Mukarram Jah and Prince Mukhaffam Jah. Some cash trusts were also created out of the proceeds of the sale of gold which had been lying idle around the palace. Some of it was packed in trunks which had remained unopened for several years. The gold was partly in the form of bars and partly in sovereigns which had been presented to him as *nazar* (offering) during his reign. The gold bars came into his hands when there was a shortage of silver in India. Currency notes were not in circulation then. Payment of the privy purse had to be in silver rupees only. The Nizam had to be paid Rs. 5,000,000 each year and in view of the shortage of silver, Sir Reginald Glancey, who handled the financial affairs of Hyderabad State, offered to pay him in gold. This was done for two years, the price of gold at that time being Rs. 21 per tola and the price of a sovereign a little over Rs. 13, the equivalent of 20 shillings sterling.

The gold was all over King Kothi. It was even under the portico of the palace, packed in covered wagons the wheels of which had sunk into the ground under the sheer weight of the gold stored inside. The whole palace knew what these wagons contained, Yet they had lain there for years under the portico without fear of being stolen. The very presence of the Nizam in King Kothi gave the gold all the protection it needed.

When it was decided that the gold should be sold, his trusted financial adviser was sent for. Collected, counted and weighed, the gold was to be taken to Bombay under special armed escort, there to be converted into cash.

The Nizam Osman Ali Khan's Jewellery

After the advent of the new regime, it became necessary to keep somewhat accurate account of the Nizam's assets. Keeping this matter in view, he decided to call Dinshah J. Gazdar, of Gazdar Ltd., the well-known Bombay jewellers, to value some of the fabulous jewellery. Gazdar's job was to present a report to the Nizam's jewellery committee on some of the objects of art and the jewellery which was the personal property of the Nizam.

Gazdar arrived in Hyderabad on 11 January 1950 and stayed a few days, during which he saw the art collection in Falaknuma Palace and the jewels in the strong room of King Kothi. He began by looking at Mogul enamels consisting of cups, plates, teapots, milk jugs, decorative parrots, *golabpashes* or rosewater sprinklers, *paan* boxes, trays, bowls. They were all studded with precious stones. He also saw four enamel elephants, a pair of camels and a horse. Next came the jades carved and set with gems, then the crystals.

The next two days Gazdar spent at King Kothi inspecting and valuing the collection of jewellery, some pieces of which were heirlooms. The strong room in which they were kept was a room approximately 120 feet long and 40 feet wide. In addition to Jacob's diamond, he saw a rare unmounted set of 22 emeralds, the total weight of which was 420 carats. The largest stone in this set was 50 carats, the smallest about 10 carats. "The colour is deep green" Gazdar later wrote in his report, "their lustre perfect."

The Nizam was in the room when Gazdar was looking over this set and he silently watched the jeweller, when Gazdar had finished his examination, the Nizam said to the jeweller, 'These I consider worth Rs. 500,000.'

Gazdar shook his head. 'No, Your Exalted Highness, I value them at Rs. 5,500,000.'

The Nizam's eyes lit up. Excitedly he shouted to the little group of officials at the other end of the room, "*Arre*, Gazdar says the emeralds are worth Rs. 5,500,000!" And all the courtiers automatically nodded their heads in agreement, as was the ritual, with their eyes popping out to show amazement. It really made little difference to the Nizam what the emeralds were worth, for it was a flea-bite in terms of his whole collection. His momentary delight was that his own conservative estimates were so completely wrong.

In the pick of the emerald collection, Gazdar included five rings, each with a square-cut, 25-carat, flawless stone and a set of armlets, the central emerald of which weighed 100 carats. There was also a most exquisite sword, richly studded with gems. Gazdar referred to this in his report as 'the permanent guardian of the ancient treasures of His Exalted Highness the Nizam.'

Exquisite Eastern jewellery was also shown to Gazdar. Of these he said: "I

Below Left
Sarpech, a turban jewel studded with over 30 emeralds.
Photograph by Prashant Panjiar, *India Today*, 1995

Below
Nizam Diamond. Glass replica. Gemological Institute of America, Carlsbad, California

Right
Baglus almas kanwal patta tilai,
the diamond and gold buckle.
Photograph by Prashant
Panjiar, *India Today*, 1995

Below
*Baglus navratan wa kanwal
almas.* Buckle studded with
different gem stones.
Photograph by Prashant
Panjiar, *India Today*, 1995

Chintak zamarrud. A necklace with emeralds and diamonds. Photograph by Prashant Panjiar, *India Today*, 1995

have never set eyes on such jewels before. Each piece is beautifully enamelled on the back in colours obtainable only after pounding precision stones. Today if I were asked to produce even a small replica of one of these I would be unable to do so, for these are unique specimens of a lost art. The Eastern jewellery collection of His Exalted Highness is one of the finest in the world, and lodged as it is in its ancestral home, it reflects the splendour of the great Asaf Jahi dynasty." Gazdar read his report to His Exalted Highness in the drawing-room of King Kothi the day before he left. Some ten or twelve palace officials were present.

When he came to the flowery sentence about the splendour of the Asaf Jahi dynasty, the Nizam excitedly clapped his hands with delight and said "Very good, very good. Please read that again." It was the romance which the jeweller wove around the jewels which appealed to the Nizam even more than their estimated value.

At the end of the four days of valuation, Gazdar rested for a while at the Rock Castle hotel, *sipping hot coffee in the cool January air.* Even so he, complained that the four enamel elephants he had seen in the showcase at Falaknuma kept dancing before his eyes and their colour was not pink. The jewels were eventually deposited in the dark and secret vaults of the Mercantile Bank on M. G. Road in the Flora Fountain business district of Bombay.

The End of an Era: Sale of the Century

In 1956, Hyderabad state was broken up into linguistic units, the Telugu-speaking areas were joined to form the new state of Andhra Pradesh. The Nizam, hitherto the titular head of the state, chose to retire from public life. He gracefully retreated into the recesses of his King Kothi palace. For the next 11 years the old man busied himself with matters concerning the welfare of his family and hangers-on. Not much was seen of Osman Ali Khan during this period. He rarely left his palace which had become an island of serenity amidst political and economic upheavals. He lost interest in the world outside the walls of the King Kothi, though the government remained ever after his wealth. During India's war with China in 1962 and with Pakistan in 1965, Osman Ali Khan was "persuaded" into donating large sums of money to the National Defence Fund. Visiting prime ministers from New Delhi sought his audience to which he agreed with the utmost reluctance. His outings were confined to the Bagh-i Aam mosque for Friday prayers and visits to his mother's grave.

In the winter of 1967 the Nizam fell ill. His grandson and successor Prince Mukarram Jah was summoned by his mother Princess Durru Shahwar to come home. In the Prince's own words as told to Warren Unna of *The Washington Post*: "I rushed into King Kothi to find people all over the place and grandfather's loose jewels and other things lying around as usual in open boxes. " On 23rd February 1967, the Nizam died after a short illness. The following day his funeral took place. Almost the entire population of the city came out on the streets to witness not merely the last journey of the Nizam but to watch for the last time the very symbol of a glorious chapter in the history of the Deccan. The *namaz-i janaza* (funeral prayer) was performed at the historic Mecca Masjid from where the dead body followed by a number of people unprecedented before and since was carried on a gun-carriage of the Indian army, to the Masjid-i Judi, where he was to be laid to rest. Amidst the sky-shattering chants of *Allahu Akbar* and *Shah Osman zindabad* , Hyderabadis buried their most beloved king, the Aala Hazrat as he was reverently called. Thousands of Hindu men and women

روزنامہ **سیاست** حیدرآباد
آندھراپردیش

نظام دکن کے شہرۂ آفاق ہیرے جواہرات، حکومت ہند کی ملکیت بن گئے

218 کروڑ روپے کا بینک ڈرافٹ نظامس جیولری ٹرسٹ کے حوالے ۔ نواب کاظم نواز جنگ کا بیان

حیدرآباد ۔15/ جنوری (سیاست نیوز) اپنے عہد کے متمول ترین انسان نظام دکن کے بیش قیمت ہیرے اور جواہرات جنکا ساری دنیا میں شہرہ تھا اب یونین آف انڈیا کی ملکیت بن گئے۔ آصف جاہی دور کے زوال کے 43 سال تک یہ ہیرے جواہرات آخری تاجدار حضور نظام میر عثمان علی خاں کے ورثہ کی ملکیت میں رہے اور بالاخر ایک طویل قانونی جنگ کے بعد جو تقریباً دو دہوں تک جاری رہی حکومت ہند کی ملکیت کا حصہ بن گئے ہیں۔ نظامس جیولری ٹرسٹ کے رکن نواب کاظم نواز جنگ (علی پاشا) نے جو آصف سابع میر عثمان علی خاں کے داماد بھی ہیں آج سیاست نیوز سے بات چیت کرتے ہوئے یہ انکشاف کیا ہیکہ ان بیش قیمت ہیرے، جواہرات کی قیمت جو 218 کروڑ روپے ہے ایک بینک ڈرافٹ کی صورت میں نظامس جیولری ٹرسٹ کو مل گئی ہے ۔ یہ ڈرافٹ بھنانے کے لئے داخل کیا گیا ہے۔ جس کے بعد رقم نظامس جیولری ٹرسٹ کے کھاتے میں آجانے گی۔ نواب کاظم نواز جنگ نے بتایا کہ اس رقم کا زیادہ تر حصہ نواب مکرم جاہ بہادر اور نواب مغنم جاہ، نواب مغنم جاہ بہادر کو ملے گا۔ انہوں نے بتایا کہ جیولری ٹرسٹ سے استفادہ کنندگان جن شخصیتوں کے نام شامل ہیں ان میں سے کئی انتقال کرگئے ہیں ۔ اسلئے انکے ورثاء انکے حصے کے مستحق ہونگے۔ جن کی تعداد اب 100 سے زائد ہوگئی ہے۔ استفادہ کنندگان کو ٹیکس بھی ادا کرنا پڑے گا۔ اسلئے ٹیکس کی منہائی کے بعد استفادہ کنندگان میں یہ رقم تقسیم کی جانے گی۔ نظامس جیولری ٹرسٹ میں نواب مغنم جاہ بہادر، جناب علی پاشاہ، محمود بن محمد، اسماعیل کانگا کے علاوہ ایک سرکاری نمائندہ شامل ہے۔ نظام جیولری ٹرسٹ نے حضور نظام کے 173 قیمتی و نایاب ہیرے، جواہرات اور موتیوں کو فروخت کرنے کی حکومت سے اجازت طلب کی تھی۔ اس میں جملہ 173 مختلف ہیرے، جواہرات ہیں۔ 1978-79 میں حکومت ہند نے ان ہیرے جواہرات کو عالمی منڈی میں فروخت کرنے کی اجازت دی تھی۔ لیکن آخر لمحہ میں فروخت پر پابندی لگادی گئی۔ تقریباً 15 سال تک حکومت ان ہیرے جواہرات کو نہ خرید رہی تھی اور نہ ہی انکی فروخت کی اجازت دے رہی تھی۔ عالمی منڈی میں ان ہیرے جواہرات کی قدر قیمت کا تخمینہ 1500 کروڑ روپے کیا گیا تھا۔ خلیج کے کئی حکمرانوں اور بروئی کے سلطان نے اس کے لئے پرکشش پیشکش کی تھی۔ سپریم کورٹ نے دو دہوں سے جاری طویل مقدمہ میں بالاخر حکومت کو یہ ہدایت دے دی کہ وہ 16/ جنوری سے قبل ان ہیرے جواہرات کو خرید لے۔ 16/ جنوری گزر جانے کے بعد نظامس جیولری ٹرسٹ کے یہ ہیرے، جواہرات فروخت کرنے کی اجازت ہوگی۔ حکومت نے مہلت ختم ہونے سے قبل ان ہیروں کو خریدتے ہوئے رقم کے ڈرافنس جیولری ٹرسٹ کو روانہ کردی۔ اسطرح دو دہوں سے جاری قانونی جنگ ختم ہوگئی۔

were observed carrying the portraits of the Nizam with sacred ash applied to his forehead.

The Nizam's grandson Prince Mukarram Jah who had been designated his successor in preference to Prince of Berar Azam Jah, took charge. After the *chahlum* (the 40-day period of mourning), Mukarram Jah was formally installed as the new Nizam in a colourful ceremony at the Chowmahalla Palace on 5th April 1967. The new Nizam faced a daunting task to put his house in order as financial matters had deteriorated due to mismanagement. In 1970, barely three years after his assumption of the rights and properties of his grandfather, Prime Minister Indira Gandhi

The news of the Nizam's jewellery sale in Hyderabad's Urdu newspaper *Siyasat* dated 16 January 1995 abolished the privy purses of all the princes, including the Nizam. This was a major blow and financial loss. After two years of inaction, Prince Mukarram Jah decided to move to Australia where he invested some money in sheep farming along with friends from Cambridge University in England, but he frequently returned to Hyderabad to look after his interests.

Along with the movable and immovable assets, Prince Mukarram Jah inherited his grandfather's fabulous jewellery. Besides Mukarram Jah there were a number of other beneficiaries of Osman Ali Khan's wealth, prominent among whom are his brother Prince Muffakham Jah and cousin Princess Fatima Fauzia, the eldest daughter of Muazzam Jah. Osman Ali Khan had willed that his jewels could be sold only after not only his own death but that of his son Prince of Berar Azam Jah which occurred in 1970. Unlike other princes and maharajas, who sold their jewels abroad for high profit, the officials of the Nizam's Jewellery Trust (NJT) suggested that the Government of India should buy the jewels as they were a national treasure. They were to bitterly regret the decision. Once the government got into the transaction the inevitable happened. It did what governments everywhere do best: delay and procrastinate. In June 1972, Prime Minister Indira Gandhi set up a committee to inspect the jewels. This committee did little beyond peeking at the jewels once. After the political changes of 1977, the NJT trustees wrote to Prime Minister Morarji Desai about the jewels. His finance minister H.M. Patel appreciated the jewels' craftsmanship but ruled out the possibility of their acquisition. From here on troubles multiplied for the Trust. A committee of the Archaeological Survey of India (ASI) examined the jewels in February 1978. The ASI declared 23 out of 89 pieces in the jewellery as antiques, which meant that they could not be exported but could only be sold to a buyer within the country. Sixty-five pieces were given non-antique certification allowing their sale and export. No decision was taken with regards to the Jacob Diamond.

Finally, after years of dilly-dallying the government announced that it did not, after all, intend to buy any of the jewels but said it would be willing to accept suitable pieces if donated or offered for display in the state museums. Understandably, the Nizam's heirs were stunned at the suggestion. This was especially so since the Trust had offered Mrs. Gandhi some land in the Chowmahalla Palace complex to start a jewellery museum, beginning with pieces from the Nizam's collection.

The NJT trustees were left with no choice but put up for sale 37 of the 65 items of jewellery cleared as non-antique. The stage was now set for the sale of the Nizam's jewellery. For three days beginning 6 March 1978, 32 leading jewellers from overseas and 38 from within India inspected the jewels and submitted tenders for each item. Among the glittering array of

Shahzadah Mukarram Jah, r. with his brother Shahzadah Mufakhkham Jah, the two major beneficiaries of the Nizam's jewellery sale. Photograph by M.A. Rahim, *Siyasat*, 1997

international jewellery firms were representatives of the house of Bulgari of Rome, Jean Rosenthal of Paris, and Winston of New York. Herbert Rosenthal of Paris who runs one of the biggest and oldest businesses worldwide in precious stones told *India Today*: "As a judge of precious stones for over 50 years, I have never seen in my life such wonderful emeralds. For their quality and their brightness the ensemble present in the sale is exquisite. Simply out of this world!" According to Sunil Sethi, *India Today*'s reporter, Rosenthal's "small eyes glinted as he spoke of the set of 22 partially-cut emeralds which weigh 414.25 carats and which were the cynosure of all trained eyes at the inspection last week." Sotheby's, the London auction house, said it would be the most expensive auction ever because the bidders were required by the court to make a minimum $26.3 million deposit in order to participate.

The jewels were about to be sold when a court order compelled the Trustees to retract. Sahibzadi Fatima Fauzia, a beneficiary, petitioned the City Civil Court in Hyderabad that the NJT trustees were not in agreement on sale as there was insufficient publicity to ensure that the heirs got the best price. An interim stay was vacated, so Fauzia appealed to the High Court. At this point Peter Jausin Fernandez, a Bangalore businessman offered Rs. 20 to 25 crores for all the 37 items, which he had not even seen. The court allowed Fernandez to inspect the jewels after submitting a deposit. After a few more legal twists and turns, the Andhra Pradesh High Court ordered that the 173 jewels should be handed over to Fernandez for Rs. 20 to 25 crores.

Now it was the turn of those who had submitted the original tenders—including the Rosenthals of Paris and Harry Winston of New York—to protest. They appealed to the Supreme Court of India, where a three-judge bench took the unprecedented decision of auctioning the jewels in the court itself. The date was fixed for 20 September 1979 and interested parties were asked to submit Rs. 20 -30 crores as earnest money. Only two—of the original 11—bidders remained in the race. One was Philip Niarchos, the 27 year old son of the Greek shipping magnate Starvros Niarchos, and the other was Mrs Badria Abdulwahab Galadari, a Dubai merchant and banker.

Both bidders were in for a rude shock. At the last minute the court was told that a cabinet sub-committee had forbidden export of the "national treasures." The auction was cancelled and the international glitterati went home empty-handed. Thereafter the matter rested in committees and legal wranglings for another decade and a half. Finally on 21st October 1994, a three-judge bench of the Supreme Court headed by Chief Justice M.N. Venkatachelliah ordered the dithering government to purchase the 173 pieces by the year-end or allow the heirs or the Nizam to sell them freely. In its 33-page order, the Court asked the government to pay the trustees 1.8 billion rupees with six percent interest from July 1991, in case it decided to buy the lot. Setting aside a valuation of $250 million to $300 million by Sotheby's and Christie's, the Court set a price equivalent to a mere $70 million.

The Government of India agreed to the Court decision. In mid-January 1995, officials of the government's Department of Culture flew to Bombay to inspect the jewels and take possession of all the 173 items at the Hong-kong & Shanghai Bank in Bombay. The high drama of the transaction saw some unusual scenes. According to Amarnath K. Menon, *India Today*'s correspondent, "when the contents of the three steel trunks were emptied onto the tables in the airless bank room in south Bombay, a hush descended on the people crowded around. The amazing lustre and exquisite craftsmanship of the Asaf Jahi rubies, emeralds, pearls, and diamonds — many in gold settings, commanded awe and admiration. Some of these items had come from the Russian czars, some belonged to Josephine, the wife of Napoleon Bonaparte. As the item-by-item inspection began, Jayant N. Chawlera, the Government's appraiser, picked up the sparkling Jacob Diamond and touched his forehead with it reverently." About the same time, on 11th January 1995, Ashok Vajpayee, the Department of Culture's Joint Secretary, arrived in Hyderabad and gave two bank drafts drawn on the Reserve Bank of India for a total amount of 2.18 billion rupees to Nawab Mir Kazim Nawaz Jang (d. 1996) known as Ali Pasha, the late Nizam's son-in-law, and Muhammad Abdul Hadi, the secretary of the NJT.

After the transaction was over in the Hongkong & Shanghai Bank, the jewels were brought to the Reserve Bank of India in Bombay under heavy escort. The same day they were flown to New Delhi in a special flight of Indian Airlines. From the airport in New Delhi the jewels were back in a bank vault, this time in the sandstone fortress that is the headquarters of the Reserve Bank of India.

For the heirs of the Nizam the settlement was bittersweet. Muhammad Abdul Hadi, said he felt some chagrin as he watched an inventory of the collection during the hand-over at the Hongkong & Shanghai Bank in Bombay. "Of course, after nearly 20 years, they were happy that there was some finality to the matter," Abdul Hadi said in a telephone conversation with John F. Burns of *The New York Times* after the sale. "But it was also an emotional, a wrenching thing," the Secretary of the Trust said of the heirs' reaction. "They were naturally disappointed that they couldn't get a better price," Abdul Hadi said, "and they were disappointed too that a big treasure that has been in the family for centuries has left for another abode." "This has been less than a fair deal," fumed Sadruddin Jhaveri, the principal advisor to Mukarram Jah. Jhaveri's reaction is understandable not only because he was an advisor to the major beneficiary of the sale, but also because he comes from a family of jewellers as his name suggests.

As soon as the sale was concluded, some of the smaller beneficiaries rushed to buy cars and apartments in Hyderabad. Dilshad Jah, one of the young beneficiaries, said "We may be able to put our lives back on the rails." Like most other heirs of the Nizam, he accused the government of giving the Asaf Jahi family a raw deal. Many of the descendants feel that they should have received the inheritance in 1973, that is three years after the death of Azam Jah, as stipulated in the Nizam's will. Instead, the trustees had to carry on a legal battle for 22 long years. The Trust had to spend a crore of rupees on the fee of legal luminaries like N.A. Palkhiwala and Soli Sorabjee. "Is this not discrimination? Did they treat the Kashmir and Jaipur royal houses similarly?" questioned Sadruddin Jhaveri, Mukarram Jah's advisor.

It is open to question whether NJT got a fair price for the jewels. Certainly they would have gotten enormously more had the jewels been sold abroad in light of Sothebys' and Christies' much higher valuation.

For instance, in 1960, a 34.64 carat pink cushion-cut diamond belonging to the Nizam was auctioned by Sotheby's in London for $128.000 to Van Cleef and Arpels, a Paris jewellery firm. It can be imagined what price the entire collection of the Nizam's jewellery would have fetched overseas today. However, the Nizam's heirs' benefit must be weighed against the immense advantage accrued to the people of India, a small yet significant part of whose natural heritage was saved from the fate met by the Koh-i-Noor, the Darya-yi-Noor, the Hope, and other diamonds.

As late as April 1997, the government of India had not taken a decision about where to display the precious objects it had purchased. Because the jewels belonged to a ruler of the Deccan, it behooves the government to deposit the jewels for permanent display in the Salar Jang Museum in Hyderabad. The choice of the Salar Jang Museum would be a fitting decision well beyond the obvious one of keeping the artifacts in their original location. It will be a wise choice also because Nawab Mir Yusuf Ali Khan, Salar Jang III, the first *Diwan* of Nizam Mir Osman Ali Khan was himself a collector of art pertaining to his native land.

Bibliography

Annotated Bibliography

The study of the Golconda diamonds and mines is poorly developed. An attempt is made here to guide scholars to the sources of further study. The guide is divided into several sections.

INTRODUCTION

An introduction to the myths surrounding the diamond and its scientific study is found in Jacques Legrand's *Diamonds: Myth, Magic, and Reality,* (New York: Crown, 1980). There are two books that can be recommended; one is by Joan Y. Dickinson, *The Book of Diamonds,* (New York: Crown, 1965), the other is The Gemological Institute of America (GIA)'s *Diamond Dictionary,* third edition, edited by Richard T. Liddicoat, (Santa Monica, CA: GIA, 1993) and its previous editions are a handy source for concise entries for various aspects of diamond.

DIAMONDS IN INDIA

No standard history exists so far, and the researcher will need to see a large number of sources. To begin, there is M.S. Shukla's *A History of the Gem Industry in Ancient and Medieval India,* (Varanasi: Bharati, 1972) and N. Viswanath's "India's Diamond Industry," *Lapidary Journal* (August 1969): 722-26. Myths current in Europe about the Golconda mines are the subject of an interesting article, which unfortunately is likely to be ignored as it is in Italian, by Daniela Bredi, "I diamanti di Golconda," *Islam storia e civilta 9,* no. 4 (1990): 253-59.

Very little is known or written about mining methods and the tools involved. In contrast the literature on the diamond trade is quite rich and varied. To begin with, see Leonard Gorelick and A. John Gwinnett, "Diamonds from India to Rome and Beyond, "American Journal of Archaeology 92 (October 1988): 547-52. A number of Persian language accounts of the time when diamond mining was still active should be consulted. Examples of the Persian works are

Tazkirat al-Muluk by Rafiuddin Ibrahim Shirazi who composed the book in 1608-11. Shirazi's manuscript located in the Salar Jang Museum library, among others, has a chapter on diamond mining in the areas of, the Adil Shahi sultanate. Toward the middle of the eighteenth century, in 1731 Lakshmi Narayan Shafiq Awrangabadi, a prolific writer and poet wrote *Khulasat al-Hind.* The manuscript is in the collection of the A. P. State Oriental Manuscripts Library. A manuscript containing fragments of village-wise revenue statistics in the Deccan is *Kitab-i dih ba dih, n.d.* but the copy is dated 1243 and located in the Andhra Pradesh State Archives (APSA). Another set of primary sources for the study of the diamond trade is in various archives. The first place to begin research is APSA which holds, among other materials, the revenue documents of the Golconda and Bijapur sultanates and the Mughals. It also holds the records of Hyderabad State and its successor state of Andhra Pradesh. See *A Guide to Persian and Urdu Records... in Andhra Pradesh State Archives*, edited by Syed Dawood Ashraf (Hyderabad: The Archives, 1993). Some facsimiles of revenue documents pertaining to the diamond mines are found in *Kitab-i Daftar-i Diwani Mal wa Mulki*, (Hyderabad: Daftar-i Diwani, 1357 A.H.) and in Selected Waqai of the Deccan 1660-1671 A.D., edited by Yusuf Husain (Hyderabad: Central Records Office, 1953). The last two works cited show the tremendous research potential APSA has in its Persian documents. Similarly useful but better organised are the papers of the European trading companies involved in the diamond trade. For the East India Company(EIC) papers see *The English Factories in India: A Calendar of Documents in India Office*, British Museum, and Public Records Office, edited by William Foster, (Oxford: Clarendon Press, 1907-27), this book covers the period 1618-1669. A book that draws heavily on the EIC records is Henry Davison Love's *Vestiges of Old Madras*, 1640-1800 3 vols., (New York: AMS Press, 1968, reprint of 1913). Walter J. Fischel, "The Jewish Merchant Colony in Madras During 17th and 18th Centuries," Journal of the Social and Economic History of the Orient 3 (1960): 78-107 and 175-95. As some of the mines were located in parts of the Qutb Shahi sultanate that eventually joined the Madras Presidency, it is useful to consult Love's book. For those who can read Dutch, there is *Dagh-Register gehonden int Casteel Batavia vant pesserende daer ter plaetse als over geheel Nederlands-India*, (The Hague: Martinus-Nijhoff, 1889-1928). Some Indian scholars have made use of the Dutch records which are replete with references to the Golconda mines. See Tapan Rayachaudhuri, *Jan Company in Coromandel, 1605-1690*, (The Hague: Martinus Nijhoff, 1962); Om Prakash, *Dutch Factories in India*, 1617-1623, (New Delhi: Munshiram Manoharlal, 1984); T.I. Poonen, "Early History of the Dutch Factories of Masulipatnam and Petapoli," Journal of Indian History, 27 (1949): 261-94; Kanakalatha Mukund, "Mining in South India in the 17th and 18th Centuries," *Indica 28, no. 1* (1991): 13-26; and Sanjay Subrahmaniam, *The Political Economy of Commerce: Southern India* 1500-1650, (Cambridge: Cambridge, University Press, 1990), and Soren Mentz, fr. from Danish by David Hohnen, English Private Trade on the Coromandel Coast, 1660-90; Diamonds and Country Trade," India Economic and Social History Review 33, no.2 (1996): 155-73.

MODERN WORKS

Some modern works based primarily on European archival sources include: Godehard Lenzen, *The History of Diamond Production and the Diamond Trade*, translated by F. Bradley, (New York: Praeger Publishers, 1966); and Gedalia Yogev, *Diamonds and Coral: Anglo-Dutch Jews and Eighteenth Century Trade*, (Leicester, England: Leicester University Press, 1978), an unusual study though strangely restricted to only one ethno-national group.

ACCOUNTS OF EUROPEAN TRAVELLERS

The Golconda diamonds were in high demand within the country and beyond in Asia and Europe. It is surprising that the diamond mines were not noticed by any Asian traveller. A number of European travellers and writers, however, have written about diamond mines though they did not actually visit the workings. See *The Book of Ser Marco Polo (1254-1323) the Venetian*, (2nd revised edition, translated and edited by Henry Yule, (London: Murray, 1875); Niccolo de Conti and Afanasii Nikitin in *India in the Fifteenth Century*, edited by R.H. Major, (London: Haklyut Society, 1857). A number of Portuguese travelogues are a reliable source of information on diamond mines in the territories of the Vijayanagara and Adil Shahi kings given the location of Goa to the west of the Deccan. See Diogo do Couta, *Decada quinta da "Asia", Book 9*, (Coimbra: Biblioteca de Universidade, 1937); Garcia da Orta, *Colloquies on the Simple and Drugs of India*, translated and edited by Robert Markham, (London: Sothern, 1913); and Fernao Nunes and Domingos Paes's *Chronica dos reis de Bisnaga*, translated by Robert Sewell as *A Forgotten Empire* Vijayanagara, (London: Swan Sonnenschein, 1900). Also relevant here is Nuno Vassallo e Silva's article, "Jewels and Gems in Goa from the Sixteenth to the Eighteenth Century," pp. 63-80, in *The Jewels of India*, edited by Susan Stronge, (Bombay: Marg, 1995) Other travelogues include: Johann Huyghen van Linschoten, *The Voyage of ... Linschoten*, 2 vols., edited by Arthur C. Burnell and Pieter Anton, (London: Haklyut Society, 1884); Joannes de Laet, *The Empire of the Great Mogul*, translated by J.S. Hoyland and S.N. Banerjee, (Bombay, 1928); Giovanni Francesco Gamelli Careri and Jean de Thevenot, *The Indian Travels of Thevenot and Careri*, edited by S.N. Sen, (New Delhi: National Archives, 1949); Thomas Salmon, 1679-1767, *Universal Traveller*, (London: J. Cooke, 1752). Some other old works referring to the Golconda diamonds are: Samuel Chappuzeau, (1625-1701), *Histoire des joyaux et de richesses de l'Orient et de l'occident=The History of Jewels...*, (London: Hobart Kemp, 1671); Karl Ritter, Die Erdekunde von Asien, 9 vols., (Berlin, 1832-59), see vol. 4 for Golconda diamonds. A review of foreign accounts is found in S. Jeyseela Stephen, "Emerging Trends of Diamond Mining... in Andhra...AD 1600-1800...", *pp. 27-54, Proceedings of seminar on Industries...* in Andhra Desa..., ed. by P. Soma Reddy etal,

(Hyderabad: Dept. of History, Osmania University, 1995).

ACCOUNTS OF VISITORS TO THE DIAMOND MINES

The factual narratives of visitors to the diamond mines constitute the most reliable source of information in the absence of scientific accounts of the mines before the late 18th century. Up until the 1980s, it was assumed that William Methwold (1590-1652) was the first known European visitor to the mines who left behind an account. In 1985, however, Prof. George Winius of the Universiteit Leiden in the Netherlands published an article on "The Life of Jacques de Couttre: A Prime Source Emerges from the Shades," Henrrario: *Bulletin of the Leiden Centre for the History of European Expansion 9*, no. 1 (1985): 136-44. Couttre visited diamond mines in Golconda and Adil Shahi territories well before anyone known to date. See *Andanzas asiaticas*, edited by Eddy Stols, B. Teensma and J. Werberckmoes, (Madrid: Historia, 1991); this is a modern version of a manuscript found in the national library of Spain. Some idea of Couttre's travel can also be gathered from Winius's "Jewel Trading in Portuguese India in the XVI and XVII Centuries," *Indica 25*, no. 1 (1988):15-34. Passages from Couttre's book in English translation can be seen in Teotonio R. de Souza's "A New Account of the Diamond Mines of the Deccan," pp. 108-123 in *Mediaeval Deccan History*, edited by A. R. Kulkarni, M. A. Nayeem, and Teotonio R. de Souza, (Bombay: Popular Prakashan, 1996), as well as in B. Teensma, "Jacques de Couttre as a Jewel Merchant in India," *Moyen Orient & Ocean Indien 7* (1990): 59-71. Dr R. J. Barendse of Leiden University is currently engaged in writing a book on the Portuguese diamond trade in the second half of the 17th century. He kindly forwarded to me the following citations as works pertinent to our subject: A Zadok Jittra, "De lotgevallen van de grote camee in het koninklijk pretenkabinet," *Oud Holland* (1951): 191-211; Francois Valentijn, *Oud en Nieuw Ost Induie*, 6 vols. (Dodrecht, 1723) and Pieter van Dam, *Beschrijvinge van de Ost-Indische Campagnie*, 7 vols. (The Hague, 1927-43.)

The second visitor to the Golconda mines was a group of three European merchants led by William Methwold (1590-1652) who went there between 1618-22. A biographical entry for him is found in the *Dictionary of National Biography*, (London: Oxford University Press, 1900-28). The account of the mines is in his *Relations of Golconda in the Early Seventeenth Century*, edited by W. H. Moreland, (London: Haklyut Society, 1931). Methwold's trip was followed some twenty years later by Jean-Baptiste Tavernier, whose account is best known given that he was both an intrepid traveller as well as a fine diamantaire. His travelogue has gone through translations in several languages. An annotated, and edited translation is by a team of a geologist and an Indologist Valentine Ball and William Crooke respectively, *Travels in India*, 2nd revised ed., (London: Oxford University Press, 1925). Charles Joret's *Jean-Baptiste Tavernier: sa vie et son oeuvre*, (Paris: Plon, 1883) is a good biography. For a reconstruction of Tavernier's route see S. Sakuntala, "Trade Routes to Kollur and Ramallakota," in her M. Phil. thesis, Dept of History, Osmania University, 1980. Many decades after Tavernier's trip, the Royal Society of London received a report in 1666 on the mines from Henry Howard, the Earl Marshal of England, who was also the sixth Duke of Norfolk. The report was published as "A Description of the Diamond Mines," *Philosophical Transactions* of the Royal Society of London 12 (1677-78): 907-17. The report has been reprinted twice with some editing and annotations by Leonard Munn, an engineer in the Nizam's service- see his "A History of the Golconda Diamond Mines," Journal of the Hyderabad Geological Survey 1, pt. 1 (1929): 21-62- and by Ramesh Chandra Sharma, "The Diamond Mines of the Deccan During the Second-Half of the Seventeenth Century," *Indian History Congress Proceedings 44* (1981): 234-50. In 1679 Streynsham Master, (1640-1724) Governor of Madras, visited the Gallapally mines while there were still in operation. See *Diaries of Streynsham Master*, 1675-1680, edited by Richard C. Temple, (London: John Murray, 1911); some extracts from the diary are reproduced by S. Krishnaswamy Iyengar, "Gollapally Diamond Mines," Journal of Indian History 9, part 3 (December 1930): 361-72. About a century after Master's visit, an East India Company official Benjamin Heyne, (1770-1819) visited visited Mallavally in 1795. His report is found in an "Account of the Diamond Mines in India," pp. 92-107, in his Tracts, Historical and Statistical in India..., (London: Black, Perry, & Co., 1814). H. W. Voysey, (1791-1824), a young geologist who has written much on the economic geology of the Deccan also wrote "On the Diamond Mines of Southern India, " Asiatic Researches 15 (1825): 120-28; for his professional accompolishments and publications see D. T. Moore, "New Light on the Life and Indian Geological Work of H. W. Voysey," Archives of Natural History 12, no. 1 (1985): 107-34.

From the early 19th century onwards we have a stream of officials and geologists making trips to the mines. For the Partiyala mines see W. Scott, "An Account of the Diamond Mines at Purtiyall," Asiatic Journal and Monthly Register 25 (1823): 228-30; for Mallavally see James Anderson, "Accounts of the Strata at the Diamond Mines of Malively," Edinburgh Philosphical Journal 3 (1820): 72-73. Valentine Ball, an eminent geologist wrote a detailed book on the economic geology of the country, see A Manual of the Geology of India, part 3, economic geology, (Calcutta: Geological Survey of India, 1881); anyone interested in pursuing detailed studies of the old diamond workings must read this seminal work. The mines at Vajrakarur (also spelled Wajrakarur) seem to have attracted a number of writers. See the following works in chronological order: T.J. Newbold, "A Glance at the Banganapilly Jaghire..." Madras Journal of Science and Literature (April 1836): 117-22, and the same author's two other works "A Cursory Notice... of Diamond Mines of Kurnool." Madras Journal of Literature and Science 11 (January 1840): 42-48;"Notes, Chiefly Geological, from Gooty to Hyderabad... Comprising a Brief Notice of the Old Diamond Pits at Dhone." Journal of the Asiatic Society of Bengal 26 (1847): 477-86. A French geologist wrote on the mines at Vajrakarur, see Maurice Chaper, "De la presence du diamant dans une pegmatite de l'Indoustan," Comptes Rendus Hebdomadaires des Seances de l'Academie des Sciences 98 (Janvier-Juin 1884): 113-15; "Sur une pegmatite a diamant et a corindon de l'Indoustan," Bulletin de la Societe Mineralogique de France 7 (1884): 47-49; and "Note sur une pegmatite diamantiere de l'Indoustan," Bulletin de la Societe Geologique de France Troisieme serie-tome Quatorzieme (1885-86): 330-45; Chaper's research was contested by R.B. Foote (d. 1912) see "Notes on Wajrakarur Diamonds and M. Chaper's Alleged Discovery of Diamonds in Pegmatite Near that Place," Records of the Geological Survey of India 22 (1889): 39-48. Foote is also the author of two related articles, "On the Geological Structure of the Eastern Coast from Latitute 15" Northward to Masulipatnam," Memoirs of the Geological Society of India 16 (1879): 1-103; and "Notes on the Geology of Parts of Bellary and Anantapur Districts," Records of the Geological Survey (GSI) of India 19 (1886): 97-111. See also Philip Lake, "The Supposed Matrix of the Diamond at Wajrakarur," Records of the Geological Survey of India 23 (1890): 69-72; the abstract of a similar paper by Charles S. Pichamuthu and S. Ramachandra Rao as "A Note on the Tuff of Wajrakarur," is found in Indian Science Congress Proceedings 19 (1932): 375.

TWENTIETH CENTURY RESEARCH AND EXPLORATION

The devoted staff of the Geological Survey of India(GSI) continues to work on prospects for diamond in Andhra Pradesh. See the following works: L.A.N. Iyer, Indian Precious Stones, revised by R. Thiagarajan in Bulletins of the GSI, series A – Economic Geology, no. 18, New Delhi: GSI, 1961; N.V.B.S. Dutt, "Ancient Diamond Mining in Andhra and its Future," Indian Minerals 7, no. 3 (July 1953): 138-50; A.K. Dey, "On the Prospects of Diamond... Mining in Andhra Pradesh," pp. 137-38, in Symposium on Mineral Industries in Andhra Pradesh Proceedings, (Hyderabad: A.P. Dept of Mines & Geology, 1963); "Exploration of Diamond,"

Indian Minerals 36, no. 4 (1982): 13-18; and S.N. Sharma, "Diamond: An Overview," Journal of Mines, Metals, and Fuels 9-10 (September-October 1985): 400-402; "Exploration for Diamonds in Andhra Pradesh," Journal of Mines, Metals & Fuels 16, no. 8 (1968): 285; C.V. Raman, "The Diamonds of the Krishna Valley," *Current Science 37*, no. 19 (1968): 541-42; not greatly different is an article by S.M. Mathur, "Diamond Mines of South India," *Gem World 2*, no. 12 (December 1975): 33-43.

A number of articles is found in *Seminar on Diamond, miscellaneous publication no. 19*, GSI, 1971: N. R. R. Ballal, "Geology of the Diamond Occurences in Andhra Pradesh," pp. 102-08; M. L. Deshpande, "Old Workings for the Diamonds in the Krishna and Districts..." pp. 176-81; and C. Karunakaran, "Exploration for Diamond in Andhra Pradesh," pp. 29-35.

N. Krishna Brahmam and S. Sakuntala, a geophysicist and a historian respectively, found "Some New Locales for Diamond Exploration in Andhra Pradesh," pp. 121-31, in *Status, Problems, and Programmes in Indian Peninsular Shield*, (Hyderabad: Institute of Indian Peninsular Geology, 1979). See also their article "Diamond Mines Near Raichur," Journal of the Geological Society of India 25, no. 12 (1984): 780-86.

A new group of geologists have advanced our knowledge of diamond exploration in Andhra Pradesh. See S.M. Mathur, "Recent Advances in Petrology, Petrochemistry and Minerology of Indian Kimberlites," pp. 44-45, in *Symposium on Three Decades of Developments in Petrology, Mineralogy and Petrochemistry in India*, Jaipur: GSI, 1981; V. Singaraju and K. Sivaji, "Quaternary and Geomorphological Studies for Diamond in Lower Sagileru Basin, Prakasam and Cuddapah Districts," *Records of the Geological Survey of India 124, part 5* (1991): 45-47; K. Sivaji and S. V. Satyanarayana, "Preliminary Surveys of Diamonds in Banganapally ..." *Records of the Geological Survey of India 124*, no. 5 (1991): 42-44; K. Prasada Rao et al, "Assessment of Diamond Resources in Kimberlites of ...Anantapur District..." *Records of the Geological Survey of India 124, no. 5* (1991): 33-

40; J. Mallikarjuna Rao and S. Nirmal Charan, "Petrography and Geochemistry of the Pipe-7 Kimberlite, Anantapur District," Journal of the Geological Survey of India 42, no. 5 (1993): 469-80; Alok K. Gupta et al "Geochemical and Microprobe Studies of Diamond-Bearing Ultramafic Rocks from Central and South India, " *Geological Society of Australia 16* (1986): 27-29. Two specialised studies deserve attention: M. L. Deshpande, "Utilisation of Hand Aungers in the Assessment of Diamond Resources in Gravel Areas, Andhra Pradesh," *Indian Minerals 30, no. 2* (1976): 22-29; and finally P.N. Chakraborty, "An Integrated Approach to Diamond Investigation in Andhra Pradesh with Special Reference to Off-Shore Areas," *Indian Minerals 33*, no.2 (1979): 24-30.

HISTORICAL WORKS

As most of the diamond mines were located in the Qutb Shahi territories, it is imperative to understand the general political and economic history of Golconda. See two standard works: H.K. Sherwani, *History of Qutb Shahi Dynasty*, (New Delhi: Munshiram Manoharlal, 1974) and John F. Richards, *Mughal Administration in Golconda*, (London: Oxford University Press, 1975) The government of A.P. published district gazetteers in which some references are found to the mines. See the volumes *Anantapur, Cuddapah, Guntur, Krishna, and Kurnool*, all published between 1967-77.

COLLECTIVE STUDIES OF INDIVIDUAL DIAMONDS

Turning to the peculiarities of Golconda diamonds and their chequered histories, see the following works beginning with Ian Balfour *Famous Diamonds*, 2nd edition. (Santa Monica, CA: GIA, 1992) and Edwin William Streeter, *The Great Diamonds of the World*, (London: Bell, 1882). Streeter was the royal gemologist to Queen Victoria. Joseph O. Gill's "A Study of Coloured Diamonds," Lapidary Journal 33, no. 4 (July 1979): 886-915 is a good start on the topic.

GOLCONDA DIAMONDS SET IN JEWELLERY

As a general introduction to jewellery in Islamic lands and India see Manuel Keene, "The Lapidary Arts in Islam," *Expedition 24, no. 1* (Fall 1981): 24-39. Susan Stronge's *Jewels of India* cited earlier is an indispensable source of information as is David N. Khalili's, short but incisive ," The Art of Mughal Jewellery," *Arts & the Islamic World* , no. 19 (Autumn-Winter 1990): 16-21. Abdul Aziz's *The Imperial Treasury of the Indian Mughuls*, (Lahore, 1942) has some interesting details on diamonds in Mogul jewellery. Herbert Tillander's *Diamond Cuts in Historic Jewellery*, (London: Art Books International, 1995) is a classic on the topic. Vivienne Becker's Golconda is a catalogue published by Hennell of Bond Street, London, in 1995. Hennell collected Golconda diamonds with old cuts and set them in contemporary designs.

Accounts of individual Historic Diamonds (in reverse chronological order)

THE KOH-I-NOOR

1994 Amini, Iradj. *Koh-i-Noor* , (New Delhi: Roli, 1994)

1993 *The Peacock Thrones of the World*, edited by K. R. N. Swami and Meera Ravi, (Bombay: Maharaja Features, 1993)

1992 Israel, Nigel B. "The Most Unkindest Cut of All: Recutting the Koh-i-Nur," The Journal of Gemmology 23, no. 23 (1992): 176.

1985 *History of Koh-i-Noor, Darya-yi Noor and Taimur's Ruby*, compiled by Nahar Singh and Kirpal Singh. (New Delhi: Atlantic Pub, 1985)

1984 Owen, Alan N. *Two of the Best Diamonds to Die For* . Connoiseur (December 1984): 168-72.

1984 Perelman, Dale Richard. *Mountain of Light*, (Winoona, MN: Apollo Books)

1982 Gill, Avtar Singh. *Maharaja and the Koh-i-Noor*,. (Ludhiana: Central Pub., 1982)

1980 Howarth, Stephen. *Koh-i-Noor Diamond: the History and the Legend.* (London: Quartet, 1980)

1979 Bhutto, Zulfiqar Ali. *If I Am Assassinated*, ed. by Pran Chopra, (New Delhi: Vikas, 1979). "As PM I demanded return of Koh-i - Noor in 1976," p. 175.

1956 Brown, J. Coggin. "The Koh-i-Nur and Babar's Diamond." *The Gemmologist* (March 1956: 50-51).

1956 Chisholm, J. R. H. "The Koh-i-Nur," *The Gemmologist* (January 1956): 7.

1955 Brown, J. Coggin. "Kollur: Reputed Home of the Koh-i-Nur," *The Gemmologist* (November 1955): 199-203; December 1955): 222-25

1953 Sen, N.D. *History of the Koh-i-Noor: The Brightest Jewel of the British Crown.* (New Delhi: New Book Society, reprinted in 1970)

1952 J. Coggin Brown, "More About Golconda," *The Gemmologist* (April 1952): 72-75.

1951 Sarkar, Jagadish Narayan, 1709-1991. *The Life of Mir Jumla, the General of Aurangzeb.* (Calcutta: Thacker, 1951) On Muhammad Saeed, known as Mir Jumla, 1591-1663, Golconda officer who defected to the Moguls. Mir Jumla was also a diamond merchant, and presented the Koh-i-Noor to Shah Jahan.

1950 F.D.S. Fripp, "The Mountain of Light, the Koh-i-Nur," Asiatic Journal n.s. 46 (April 1950): 998-1010.

1948 Faruqi, Muinuddin Rahbar. Koh-i-Noor ki Sarguzasht., (Hyderabad: Azam Steam Press, 1948)

1934 Smith, Vincent Arthur, On the Identity of the Great Mogul's Diamond with the Koh-i-Noor, forms the Appendix II in *Travels in the Mogul Empire* by Francois Bernier, translated by Archibald Constable, (London, 1934)

1907 Manucci, Niccolao. *Storia do Mogor or Mogul India*, 1653-1708, translated with introduction & notes by William Irvine, (London: John Murrary, 1907).

1899 Beveridge, Henry, *Babar's Diamond: Was it the Koh-i-Nur?* Asiatic Quarterly Review 7 (January-April 1899): 370-89.

1895 Streeter, Edwin W. *The Koh-i-Nur Diamond: Its Romance and History* (London: George Bell & Sons; reprinted from Streeter's earlier work with some additional material.

1893 Burton, Isabel, *The Life of Sir Richard Burton* , (London: Chapman & Hall, 1893), see the chapter :The Koh-i Noor," pp. 94-97.

1891 Maskelyne, N. Story, "The Koh-i-Nur: A Criticism," *Nature* (8 October 1891): 555-59. Valentine Ball's response in the same journal's issue dated 12 October 1891: 592-93.

1890 Ball, Valentine, "The Great Mogul's Diamond and the Koh-i-Noor," Nature (4 December 1890): 103.

1852 "The Koh-i-Noor." The Illustrated London News (18 September 1852): 213.

1852 Brewster, David, "Observations of the Diamond." The Athenaeum (18 September 1852): 1014.

1851 "Koh-i-Noor," Magasin Pittoreque, (1851): 504-505.

1850 "Great Diamond." Littell's *Living Age* (Boston) 26, no. 327 (24 August (1850): 345-46.

THE HOPE DIAMOND

1991 Hubbord-Brown, Janet. *The Curse of the Hope Diamond.* New York: Avon, 1991)

1976 *Blue Mystery: The Story of Hope Diamond.* (Washington, DC: Smithsonian Institution, 1976)

1975 Tillander, Herbert. *The "Hope" Diamond and its Lineage*, (Helsinki, 1975)

1921 *The Hope Diamond Mystery.* (Film) Howells Sales Company. Darya-yi Noor and Other Diamonds Stolen & Taken to Iran

1994 Jellicoe, Patricia, "Crown Jewels", in *Encyclopedia Iranica* , (Costa Mesa, CA: Mazda, 1994)

1994 Doka, Yahya, "Darya-ye Nur," *Encyclopedia Iranica*, (Costa Mesa, CA: Mazda, 1994)

1992 'Tehran Journal: With New Pride Iran Dusts off the Crown Jewels,' The New York Times 8 May 1992:A4. Including the Darya-yi Nur at Bank-i Milli.

1989 Taqizadeh, S.-H. Zindagi-i Tufani, ed. by Iraj Afshar, (Tehran, 1989)

1968 Meen, V.B., A.D. Tushingham, and G.G. White, "Long Lost Darya-i Nur Largest Pink Diamond Rediscovered: The Darya-i Nur Diamond and the Tavernier 'Great Table'," The Lapidary Journal 21, no. 8 (1968): 1000-1009.

1968 Meen, V.B. et al. Crown Jewels of Iran , (Toronto: University of Toronto Press, 1968)

1921 Jamalzadeh, M. A. "Koh-i Noor, Darya-yi Noor," *Kava 2*, no. 2 (1921): 5-8.

1833 Brydges, Harford J. *The Dynasty of the Kajars* , (London: John Bohn, 1833). Saw the Darya-yi Nur

OTHER SIGNIFICANT DIAMONDS

"Almaz Shakh" *Izvestiyakh Rossiskoi Akademii Nauk series 6*, vol. 16 (1922): 451-62. On Shah diamond.

Balfour, Ian. "A Magnificent Historical Diamond," pp. 235-42, in *Magnificent Jewels, auction catalogue,* (Geneva: Christie's, 15 November 1995). On Ahmadabad diamond.

Catalogue of Highly Important Jewels Including the Two Historic 'Arcot' Diamond, auction catalogue, London: Sotheby's, June 25, 1959.

Ball, Valentine, "On the Identity of Some Ancient Diamonds in India, Especially Those Mentioned by Tavernier," Nature (24 March 1881): 490-91.

Dalton, Cornelius N. *The Life of Thomas Pitt*, (Cambridge: Cambridge University Press, 1915) Regarding Pitt-Regent diamond.

McGlashan, Ian, "The Pigot Diamond," Lapidary Journal (January 1979): 2300-2302.

Marshall, P.J. "The Personal Fortune of Warren Hastings," The Economic History Review 17, no. 2 (1964): 284-300.

Sokrovishcha Almasznogo fonda SSSR= *Treasures of the USSR Diamond Fund*, (Moscow: Sovtskii Khudozhnik, 1967)

Suri, Sanjay, "Long Lost Indian Gem Fetches $4.3 Million," India Abroad (New York, 24 November 1995): 52. On Ahmadabad diamond.

Tillander, Herbert, "Another Brief Look at the

Sancy Diamond," The Journal of Gemmology 26, no. 4 (October 1978): 221-28.

Tolanksy, Samuel, 1907-73. "The Great Table Diamond of Tavernier," The Journal of Gemmology 3, no. 5 (January 1962).

Waite, G.G. "The Orloff and Tavernier's Great Mogul Diamond," Lapidary Journal 26, no.1 (1972): 32-33.

DIAMONDS IN FICTION AND FILM

Diamonds in the temple idols seem to be of interest to novelists and film-makers. Wilkie Collins (1824-89)'s *Moonstone*, (New York: Harper, 1868) is considered the first detective novel involving an Indian diamond set in the "eye" of a goddess. The plot of this novel is closely followed in *The Quest of the Sacred Jewel*, a film directed by George Fitzmaurice. Similarly, *A Prince of India* is a film about a diamond which fatally curses all who possess it, save the rightful owners. See also entries under Idol's Eye in various diamond dictionaries. For the sale in the United States a diamond of the same name, see "Idol's Costly Eye," see *Life* (18 January 1963): 49.

THE NIZAM'S WEALTH AND JEWELLERY

1848 Piddington, Henry, and Captain George Fleetwood Charles Fitzgerald, 1808-88. "On the Great Diamond in the Possession of the Nizam," Journal of the Asiatic Society of Bengal 17, part 1 (January-June 1848): 151-53.

1876 Burton, Richard F., 1840-1922. "The Nizam Diamond," Quarterly Journal of Science 6 (1876): 351-60.

1925 Nadawi, Ikramullah Khan, Wiqar-i Hayat, (Aligarh, 1925) For Jacob diamond case.

1953 Brinda, Maharani of Kapurthala. The Story of an Indian Princess (New York: Henry Holt, 1953. References to the Nizam Osman Ali Khan gifts of diamonds to the princess.

1955 Karaka, D.F., 1911-75. *Fabulous Mogul: Nizam VII of Hyderabad*, (London: Verschoyle, 1955). Informal but extremely readable biography.

1955 "Household Money of the Nizam," Newsweek (New York, 12 September 1955): 46. On the loss of currency notes worth $8.4 million eaten up by rats.

1967 "The Nizam's Unassessed Wealth," Link (New Delhi, 6 August 1967): 18.

1967 Unna, Warren, "New Nizam Pinches Rupees," The Washington Post (27 August 1967): B5.

1978 Sethi, Sunil. "Nizam's Purse," India Today (16-31 March 1978): 13.

1979 Nizam's Jewel Auction Fails to Come Off," The Times of India (Bombay, 21 September 1979):1.

1984 Allen, Charles, and Sharada Dwivedi, *Lives of Indian Princes*, (London:Century Publishing, 1984) References to the Nizam's pearl collection.

1988 Menon, Amarnath K. "Hidden Treasure: A precious Private Collection of Jewellery Lies buried in a Bank Vault," India Today (New Delhi, 30 April 1988): 100-101.

1991 Ram Murthy, S. "11-Kg Priceless Gold Coin Missing," The Deccan Chronicle (5 January 1991): 1.

1995 Rahman, G. "All Nizam Trust Beneficiaries are not Equally Lucky," Saudi Gazette (Jeddah 19 January 1995): 9.

1995 Basu, Nupur. "Government to Protect Hyderabad Heritage," India Abroad (New York, 27 January 1995): 38.

1995 Burns, John F. "Crown Jewels of the Nizam: All are India's Now," The New York Times (2 February 1995): A:4.

1995 Panjiar, Prashant, and Amarnath K. Menon, "Nizam's Jewels: Worth a King's Ransom," India Today (15 February 1995): 68-75.